HARVARD HISTORICAL MONOGRAPHS, LXX

Published under the direction of the Department of History
from the income of the Robert Louis Stroock Fund

GEORGE HENRY LEWES

From *Popular Science Monthly,* 9 (1876)

GEORGE HENRY LEWES:

A VICTORIAN MIND

HOCK GUAN TJOA

(1)

HARVARD UNIVERSITY PRESS

CAMBRIDGE, MASSACHUSETTS, AND LONDON, ENGLAND

1977

Library of Congress Cataloging in Publication Data

Tjoa, Hock Guan, 1943-
George Henry Lewes.

(Harvard historical monographs; 70)
Bibliography: p.
Includes index.
1. Lewes, George Henry, 1817-1878.   I. Series.
B1593.Z7T59   192   77-8610
ISBN 0-674-34874-5

Preface

George Henry Lewes ranks with Bagehot, Hutton, and Leslie Stephen among the better practitioners of Victorian higher journalism. Of the four, only Hutton remains without a more or less complete biographer or expositor. Lewes himself has been well served by Gordon Haight's solid biography of George Eliot and magnificent edition of her letters, which also contains hundreds of Lewes'. There have been a few dissertations on Lewes, as well as published accounts of his literary criticism and a bright vignette in John Gross's *Rise and Fall of the Man of Letters*. I have not therefore attempted a comprehensive Life and Works, but rather an analysis of Lewes' major intellectual preoccupations, which I believe were moral and philosophical. He pursued an understanding of the fundamental and universal "structures" of life and thought with an earnestness which should surprise no one even casually acquainted with the novels of George Eliot and with the fact of their twenty-four year companionship. This aspect of Lewes' thought and work has not been examined adequately. To dwell upon his serious intellectual concerns does some injustice to his reputation for vivacious conversation and sparkling prose, particularly that of his articles written in the eighteen-forties and fifties, but these grave tendencies reflect such an important sub-

stratum of Victorian intellectual life that I have felt justified
in dealing almost exclusively with them. I have, however,
placed before this analysis a discussion of the social setting
of his journalistic career because it appeared necessary, if
only as a corrective to the cherished platitudes of Victorian
conventional wisdom, to take cognizance of the circumstances within which a man of letters advanced his career.
To a certain extent these circumstances left a permanent
mark on Lewes; after so many years devoted to essays and
reviews, he was not entirely at home writing treatises.

This study began as a dissertation submitted to the Department of History, Harvard University. Readers wishing
more complete documentation or a more extended treatment of the subject may consult the original typescript in
the Harvard University Archives.

It is a pleasure to acknowledge the unfailing guidance
and helpful criticism of Professor John L. Clive, who super-
vised my thesis, and of Professor Donald Fleming, who
also read it as it was being written. I am grateful to Professor
H. J. Hanham for answering questions about Lewes and the
Victorian profession of letters, and to Professor Robert L.
Wolff for general discussions on Victorian novels. The
Senior Common Room of Mather House provided a welcome variety of intellectual companionship; to Professor
Samuel H. Beer and the other members of the staff of Social
Sciences 2, 1968-1971, I am deeply indebted for three years
of widely ranging intellectual stimulation. Professor Gordon
S. Haight made many helpful comments and suggestions
when this study began as a thesis and again when it was re-
written; no one who works on a Victorian subject can fail to
appreciate how much I owe to him. Finally, this work has
been vastly improved by Mrs. Sidney Gleason's conscientious
exposure of error and infelicity. I hope I have made ade-

quate acknowledgment of the more obvious of my intellectual debts in the notes to this work. Needless to say, no one other than myself is responsible for its shortcomings.

The staffs of the Harvard College Library, the Boston Athenaeum, the Boston Public Library, the Beinecke and Sterling libraries at Yale University, the Berg Collection of the New York Public Library, the British Museum, the Cambridge University Library, the Archives Positivistes, Paris, and the University of Malaya Library all responded with courtesy and generosity to my many requests. Grants from the Department of History and from the Center for West European Studies, Harvard University, enabled me to consult materials away from the immediate vicinity of Cambridge, Massachusetts, and to make my research more complete. And, without the generous fellowship aid of the Harvard-Yenching Institute, I would not have been able to undertake any graduate study at Harvard at all.

Kuala Lumpur

Contents

GEORGE HENRY LEWES

1 / The Making of a Man of Letters

What we did we were, What we can do we are.
George Henry Lewes

George Henry Lewes was not a member of the Victorian "intellectual aristocracy"; indeed, one biographer labeled him a "miscellaneous writer."[1] Unlike Macaulay, Huxley, Arnold, Darwin, or Leslie Stephen, he did not come from a family which produced a striking number of eminent Victorians. Yet he insisted, as did many liberal intellectuals of his day, that there was an aristocracy of talent as well as an aristocracy of birth, and in the aristocracy of talent Lewes secured a place for himself. He was gifted with an ability to learn quickly and to apply his knowledge imaginatively; his capacity for work, like that of many of his contemporaries, beggars the imagination, and he found in the higher journalism of mid-nineteenth-century England the opportunities that he needed. His was not the sort of heroic genius that catapulted Dickens, Carlyle, or George Eliot from obscurity to the heights of the aristocracy of talent. He had some profound insights, and he put things together rather well, but the major portion of his success was achieved through a prolific and versatile journalism that was characteristic of his time; the age of Johnson had given way to the age of the scribbling set. Victorian England was not lacking in genius, of course, but the most salient features of its intellectual life were the numerous high-quality periodicals of general culture and the host of lesser, second-order minds that contributed to them.

The Victorians themselves tended to ascribe success entirely to character and usually ignored the circumstances that surrounded a man's life and career; they hardly ever paid as much attention to general factors as they did to individual virtues. The moralism that so pervaded Victorian attitudes demanded that an individual be totally responsible for his doings and, by extension, for his station in life. Lewes did pause to wonder if Goethe's character, his serenity and his dislike of politics, might not have been the result of the middlingness of his social origins,[2] but his own first novel revealed his true sentiments. In *Ranthorpe* (1847) he purported to portray the career of a young poet, and his descriptions of the hopes, stragagems, and struggles of literary life seemed authentic to Poe, who thought highly of that novel. Lewes' main concern was in fact the moral character of his hero, and he ascribed Ranthorpe's failure in art to a moral defect, presumption: "Born a member of the great aristocracy of intellects, he misconceived his rank, and yearned for recognition and fellowship in the great aristocracy of birth." The success of his first volume had gone to his head and Ranthorpe allowed himself to be carried away by the capricious lionization of the fashionable world. He found no peace and wrote no more until he came to himself and returned to his true position in society, as symbolized by his marriage to his childhood sweetheart.

Despite its superiority to *Ranthorpe* as art and as a social document, Thackeray's *History of Pendennis* (1848) also betrayed the fact of its middle-class provenance by a similar reduction of *Künstlerroman* to *Bildungsroman*. Again, the hero's artistic potential was jeopardized by moral weakness—like Ranthorpe's, a susceptibility to the flesh pots of "fashionable life." But this gospel of character and self-help masks important social conditions. For instance, a study of more than a thousand British authors whose reputations were made between 1800 and 1930 reveals certain interesting circumstances. About ninety per cent of these authors came from the "middle-middle" class, rather than from the wealthy upper-middle class which might in time have inched its way into the upper classes or from the lower-middle class of tradesmen and artisans who were often indistinguishable from the lower classes. Secondly, these literary men and women did not come from the increasingly numerous commercial sector of the middle class (ship-builders, or manufacturers, or insurance agents), but had fathers who were either clergymen or members of the "arts and professions," which included teachers, lawyers, doctors, civil servants, and artists. Furthermore, most of these men and women of letters were educated either in upper-class grammar schools or in their middle-class imitations, the private-venture schools, rather than in the utilitarian institutions set up by the nonconformists. The education of Victorian littérateurs, therefore, was largely traditional and classical. In a sense, they were equipped to mediate between Culture, which had been an almost exclusively aristocratic preserve, and the middle class which became increasingly interested in it.[3]

Professor Altick's study of authorship thus gives concrete data in support of those impressions one might have gained from a reading of the lives of men of letters. Trollope's mother was a literary personage in her own right, and Trollope remembered her love for Dante, Spenser, and Byron, and her familiarity with literature in general. Lewes himself recalled the delight with which he and his brother would steal away from home into a theater. On the other hand, when Samuel Smiles, as a child of commercial middle-class parents, expressed a wish to become a painter, his mother thought he meant a house painter and would hear nothing more of that.[4] And so, instead of adding his vision to the Victorian perception of the physical universe, Smiles went on to write the *Lives of the Engineers, Self-Help,* and other works which crystallized certain important aspects of the moral universe of the Victorians. It is apparent, then, that whatever the Victorians as individuals and as a society might have wanted to believe about the triumph of character over circumstances, certain social conditions laid down general constraints on a man's career and achievements.

The argument for the weight of circumstances is reinforced by the revelation that, like Lewes, a sizeable number of the authors in Altick's study derived their principal support from journalism (as opposed to living on royalties from books). Only when a large number of journals existed could this have been possible. In the first two decades of the nineteenth century, this was not the case, as Carlyle and Leigh Hunt discovered, for only about thirty new periodicals were begun in each decade. Between 1821 and 1830, however, over a hundred magazines were started in London alone. And the numbers increased steadily until the 1860's when new ventures hit the high of 170; the *Newspaper Press Directory* for 1865 recorded 554 periodicals. Many were trade journals, and most of the rest offered mainly light fiction in serial form. Of these, Dickens' *Household Words* (1850-1859) and *All the Year Round* (1859-1895) were among the best known and better flavored, though Dickens himself defended the sensationalistic and "coarsely seasoned" as providing much-needed diversion for an overworked population. There was, in addition, an increase in the publication of periodicals of culture and opinion, the so-called higher journalism, which provided so much scope for the would-be

men of letters. This increase in the publication of news-
papers, trade journals, and periodicals of a literary, philosophic, or religious nature was partly due to the increase in
population and in the literacy rate in the first half of the
nineteenth century. Indeed, the spread of literacy to the
working class was a cause for some alarm as reflected in the
Government's extreme reluctance to lower the "taxes on
knowledge" and in the attempt of those like Henry
Brougham and Charles Knight who tried to induce the
embourgeoisement of the working class.[5]

The larger part of the demand for periodicals was a function of increasing prosperity: trade journals became more
necessary, and conditions for reading improved with more
leisure and better provision for lighting. Reading interest
was aroused by the tremendous appeal of Scott's novels and
Byron's poems. Dramatic social and political developments
—the Napoleonic Wars, the Reform Bill, the Poor Law, the
Factory Act, the tremendous effort put into the mobilization
of opinion and moral indignation against slavery and later
against the Corn Laws—all led to a heightened political
awareness on the part of the public and to an increasing
demand for information. Religious interests, too, stimulated
periodical publication, and in the early nineteenth century
matters of perennial sectarian concern were refreshed and
reinforced by larger issues such as Catholic Emancipation,
the Oxford Movement, and, a little later, Science and Rationalism. Early Victorian readers demanded to be entertained, and an incredible amount of fiction gushed forth;
they asked to be informed, and so they were; they sought to
be kept abreast of intellectual developments as well, and an
army of miscellaneous writers marched forth to plunder all
fields and returned displaying the loot in innumerable
reviews.

Unlike the readers of an earlier age who could afford to

spend a guinea or more on their reading material, the bulk
of the Victorian readership was made up of artisans or clerks
who might have a shilling or two to spend. They more than
made up for their lack of means by their number, but they
were also less able to comprehend the original writers of
their time. Thus mass culture emerged. The ten-pound
voters required a semi-digested literature, hence the growing demand for periodicals containing reviews, summaries,
digests, and aids.[6] Much of this kind of journalism consisted
of nothing but hack work, for the mass of the reading public
then was not more discerning than it is today. The writers
often got paid for quantity and topicality rather than
quality or originality. Much of Lewes' earlier writing bore
the marks of inexperience and haste, and was heavily padded
— the consequence of his need to make a living. Unlike some
of his fellow littérateurs, he did not have independent means
or a position in the civil service, in the church, or on the edi-
torial board of one of the better journals. Nor had he yet
obtained the financial and professional security of the successful author. But he had the right background and the
appropriate training, and he chose the most rewarding
avenue for making a career in letters.

Very little is known of George Henry Lewes' father, John
Lee Lewes; his paternal grandfather, however, was a well-
known harlequin with the Drury Lane Theatre. Charles Lee
Lewes, son of a hosier and part-time messenger in London,
was proud "of being the scion of as honest a Cambrian as
ever ranked with the reputable tradesmen of this kingdom,
but whose classical education qualified him for the circle of
polite arts," such as that of Dr. Young, the author of *Night
Thoughts*. As a result of this exposure to classical education
his sisters were able to become governesses, but Charles him-

self did not follow such conventional steps to social better-
ment.[7] Instead, he went on the stage, where he was successful enough to have merited a notice in the *Dictionary of
National Biography*. John, who was perhaps also an actor,
had strong literary inclinations and published, in addition
to his father's *Memoirs,* two volumes of verse: *Poems*
(1811) and *National Melodies* (1817). The list of subscribers
to the second volume included theater people, members of
the Royal Navy, and the Duke of Marlborough. Thus the
efforts begun by the hosier and continued by his descendants
succeeded in raising the family into the middle class and
into that segment of it which enjoyed some semblance of
gentility and culture. There were, in addition, prudent
marriages. Charles's mother was related to Sir John Gilford
Lawson and, distantly, to the dowager Lady St. Aubyn. He
himself married three times, and his first two wives — nothing
is known of the third — were wealthy enough to have left
property to their respective children. John Lee inherited
enough to support a style of life which gained him the nick-
name, "Dandy Lewes." He died when George was two years
old, but his wife somehow managed through seven years of
widowhood until her marriage to John Willim, a retired
captain of the 18th Native Infantry Regiment in Bengal.
George himself did quite well in marrying Agnes Jervis, the
beautiful daughter of Swynfen Jervis who in 1837 was M.P.
for Bridport, Staffordshire. In the early years of their marriage her inheritance helped eke out his literary earnings.[8]

George Lewes was thus of the comfortable middle class. If
Percy Ranthorpe, the hero of his first novel, nearly starved
himself in order to be able to afford a sixpenny volume of
Shelley, that was perhaps a literary convention understandable in the Romantic Age, for Lewes himself found the
wherewithal to pay twenty shillings for a copy of *Spinozae*

Opera Posthuma. Nor did he trudge snail-like to school, like Shakespeare or Anthony Trollope—years later he was able to recall the wheels which whirled him to school and to extol the joys of a coach ride. William Bell Scott, who found him in 1837 living quietly and comfortably with his family, said: "I have seen it stated that he denied himself food to enable him to purchase books, but no symptom of any such necessity was visible about the *ménage,* nor do I believe it ever existed."[9]

Lewes' education, too, was quite sound, although from the lofty heights of the intellectual aristocracy Leslie Stephen pronounced it "desultory." Not everyone could get into one of the nine ancient grammar schools, and the local grammar schools were in a sorry state. Nor were the ancient schools, unreformed as yet, particularly desirable: Thackeray was unhappy at Charterhouse, and Trollope was positively miserable at Harrow. Instead, Lewes was sent to various private-venture schools—in Boulogne, Britanny, and St. Helier on the island of Jersey. This early exposure to France and French culture was useful to Lewes' career for he was able to draw on his knowledge of French literature in writing for the various reviews. He finished his secondary schooling at an institution in Greenwich, run by the Rev. Dr. Charles Parr Burney. It was, Frederick Locker-Lampson recorded, "a huge unregenerate school" which had once been famous, for Dr. Burney was the grandson of Johnson's friend, the music historian. Though the school was unregenerate, the severe *Athenaeum* reported that Dr. Burney enjoyed the "not unmerited reputation of 'grounding' his pupils thoroughly in classical knowledge," which was perhaps more than could have been said of the unreformed public schools.[10]

Unlike an increasing majority of his fellow littérateurs,

however, Lewes did not go to university. While this was not a severe handicap, it appears to have made him sensitive to any criticism that implied a lack of intellectual worth in his writings. When, for instance, Carlyle asked Lewes in 1852 if anyone read his pieces on Comte in the *Leader*, a radical weekly he edited jointly with Thornton Hunt, Lewes reportedly "bridled" and claimed that indeed they did, especially at Oxford. There was some interest in Comte at Oxford at that time, though Benjamin Jowett thought that "it was a poor thing to have studied all philosophies and to end in adopting that of Auguste Comte."[11] Furthermore, when Huxley, reviewing Lewes' work on Comte for the *Westminster Review* in 1854, suggested that he made errors "not excusable even on the plea of mere book-knowledge," Lewes waxed eloquent in indignation at what he thought was a charge of amateurism. Huxley's attack,

being founded on the natural but false assumption that, because Literature is my profession, therefore in Science I can only have "book knowledge" it will fall in with the all but universal tendency of not allowing any man to be heard on more than one subject. Once for all let me say that it is eighteen years since I first began to occupy myself — practically and theoretically — with Biology, and that it is only within the last four years that I have ventured to publish any opinions on that subject. [12]

Lewes was exaggerating; in 1859 he recalled the beginning of his friendship with Spencer in 1851 as the stimulus that roused his "dormant love of science."[13] Huxley subsequently reevaluated Lewes' scientific achievement especially after the publication of *Sea-side Studies* (in 1856-1858), but his earlier criticism was a sign of the times. It was becoming more difficult for autodidacts, however gifted, to enter the various fields of science which were becoming ever more specialized and technical. In 1818, at the age of thirty-three, Adam Sedgwick had been named Woodwardian Professor of Geology at Cambridge without knowing anything about the subject. When Lewes turned to science in the 1850's as an amateur, he found only moderate success, for the pace of research and publication had stepped up considerably. The opening of London University had marked, among other things, a great step forward in professional education in England, and the establishment of the natural sciences tripos at Cambrige in 1853, in a way, signaled the end of amateurism in science. Even the study and criticism of literature became more and more professional and academic towards the end of the nineteenth century. Had Lewes been born a generation later, his career would have had to have been quite different.

Some time in the mid-1830's Lewes "walked the wards." The medical profession did not generally pay well, as Samuel Smiles could testify, but since it required more skill than patronage, it offered better prospects for advancement than the church or the army. Both George and his brother Edward, therefore, as members of the advancing middle class, took up medicine. Edward pursued his medical education to the end. Had George done so, he might have felt more secure about his standing as a scientist, but he was troubled by the sight of pain, something which he later claimed hampered his physiological research. He maintained an interest in science, however, especially in what we would call the life sciences, and in the 1850's engaged in seaside explorations and microscopical studies. After George Eliot's success added to their financial security in the following decade, he was able to indulge his philosophical and scientific interests even further, working more exclusively on the problems of defining life and mind and making special trips to the Continent to visit laboratories and to consult various experts such as Hermann von Helmholtz and Wilhelm Wundt on points of physiology and psychology.

Despite his stints as a medical student and as clerk for a merchant, Lewes' first efforts in journalism were literary. In this respect, he was well prepared, with a good grounding in the classics, an early interest in the theater, and a familiarity with France and the French language. In the hope of "breaking" into journalism, Lewes began by sending pieces of his work to various reviews and to such eminent men of letters as Leigh Hunt, who had a great deal of experience with the better periodicals both as a writer and as an editor. The personal intervention of someone already in the field seems to have been essential. Trollope's pieces on Ireland made no impact when submitted to the *Examiner;* Francis Espinasse found Carlyle's influence necessary; Leslie Stephen's way was smoothed over by his brother FitzJames. It was Leigh Hunt who appears to have been Lewes' patron. When Lewes was only seventeen, he sent a poem and a short story to Hunt. Some of Lewes' earliest pieces appeared in the *Monthly Repository* during Hunt's editorship (June 1837 to April 1838) of that important, formerly Unitarian magazine, and his lectures in 1837 at the Finsbury chapel of W. J. Fox, a former editor of the magazine, were probably also arranged through Hunt's good offices.

They became close friends. In 1838, when George was in Germany for a prolonged stay, he wrote back claiming to have made a "prodigious host of acquaintances" while studying by day and spending his evenings at concerts, at the theater, or in society; nevertheless, he missed the "champagne evenings" in Hunt's study: "We sitting opposite each other over the fire ransacking the worlds of literature and philosophy for food, your fine, earnest face *looking* a treatise on Aesthetics — your gentle and delicate reproofs of my folly, impetuosities and one-sided news." Lewes reported jubilantly that Karl August Varnhagen von Ense, the German statesman turned literary critic, had compared Hunt to Goethe. Two years later Lewes referred to a similar comparison between Hunt's *Ralph Esher* and Goethe's *Wilhelm Meister:* "I am convinced," he wrote reproachfully, "that you could if you chose write a *Wilhelm Meister* and the good you would do you know well." Upon the death of Wordsworth, Lewes — by that time the literary editor of the *Leader* — stoutly argued that Hunt was the only worthy choice for poet laureate.[14]

Lewes may well be forgiven his exuberant faith in Hunt; some years later his ardor cooled considerably. But Hunt's help at the beginning of his career was indispensable. It was probably Hunt who introduced him to Carlyle, a neighbor in Cheyne Row, and to John Stuart Mill, both of whom helped him generously. Mill had to chide Lewes for being a "conjurer" in searching out his old papers and referring to them; Lewes no doubt intended this as a gesture of discipleship, but his directness and energy made him suspect in some circles. Mill, however, assured Macvey Napier that Lewes' apparent presumption was really a commendable willingness to try to do more than he could, which Mill thought the best way to improve one's abilities, and he argued that, withal, Lewes was more than willing to listen to criticism.[15] Other young, aspiring men of letters, such as David Masson and Alexander Bain, found Mill generous with his time and advice. For Lewes, he willingly discussed literary and philosophical problems, and wrote letters of introduction to various publishers and editors and to French intellectuals like Tocqueville and Victor Cousin.

Lewes' interest in philosophy and positivism was confirmed in the early forties, during the period when he had most contact with Mill. They discussed the later volumes of Comte's *Cours de philosophie positive* (1830-1842) as they appeared, and also Mill's *System of Logic* (1843). Mill thanked Comte for receiving Lewes, and kept him informed of the latter's progress in positivism, "notre doctrine commune."[16] Lewes concluded his *Biographical History of Philosophy* (1845-1846) with a brief but enthusiastic chapter on Comte, whom he hailed as the Bacon of the nineteenth century, the new unifier of a new form of knowledge. Comte took offense at Lewes' independent views in his essays on positivism in the *Leader* (1852) and was especially annoyed at Lewes' assertion that the *Système de politique positive* (1851-1854) was not "positive." Lewes maintained throughout his career that he was a reverent heretic and was later (around 1866) converted by George Eliot to the view that the *Système* was indeed a positivist utopia.[17] Though the Leweses were warm friends of such positivists as the Richard Congreves and Frederic Harrison, they never gave more than moral and token material support to the Positivist movement.

Lewes' acquaintance with Carlyle added a different dimension to his intellectual interests. It began at least as early as 1839 when Lewes visited Varnhagen in Berlin with an introduction from the Sage of Chelsea. In a moment of deep gratitude, when it appeared that Carlyle was one of the few people who understood his marital problems and sympathized with his going to Weimar with Marian Evans, Lewes fervently recalled that he had sat at Carlyle's feet while his mind was "first awakening." Some of his essays written in the early 1840's contained what Mill considered to be excessive Carlylisms—a common and understandable occurrence, after all, in the decade after *Sartor Resartus*.[18] On one occasion Lewes went to Carlyle to see if he had a good word for *Rose, Blanche, and Violet* (1848), his second novel. Carlyle remained firmly noncommittal, preferring to discuss the recent Chartist disturbance at Kensington Common (April 10, 1848). It was perhaps an act of kindness as well, for Carlyle's annotations show that he thought Lewes' writing artificial and inflated; to Mrs. Carlyle the annotations were the only amusing things in the book.[19] It was Carlyle, however, who by teaching and by example stimulated interest in German thought among his "good young friends." He urged upon them the study of Kant, "the prime author of the new spiritual world," over the claims of Fichte, Schelling, and Hegel. Kant, he believed, would provide the antidote to the "fatal incubus of Scotch or French philosophy, with its mechanisms and its Atheisms."[20] Lewes' *Biographical History of Philosophy* reflects an interest in German philosophy that deepened through its successive editions.

By 1852, Lewes claimed, he had been to Germany no fewer than five times. There he found a new perspective in literary criticism, which he proceeded to expound, with varying effect, in articles on Hegel, Goethe, A.W. Schlegel, and Lessing. In Vienna he met Liszt, with whom he struck up a lasting friendship. And in Berlin he heard Schelling lecture and "gained knowledge" of Hegel by talking to the philosopher's editors and friends. But Lewes' first publication on Goethe (1843) did not please Carlyle: it was the common, philistine view of Goethe, for, like many of his compatriots, Lewes felt uncomfortable with the detachment of the German genius and took it for coldness and lack of political or moral earnestness.[21] Over the next twelve years, during which he saw much of Carlyle, Lewes did further research and thinking on Goethe, and his full-scale biography was a mature, comprehensive, and sensitive work of which

Carlyle thoroughly approved. The formidable Margaret Fuller was at a dinner party at Carlyle's while Lewes was still working towards the biography of Goethe, and she thought him "French," flippant, and too shallow and irreligious for such a task. But she was glad for his anecdotes and his ability to interrupt Carlyle, who was in a particularly grim mood. Lewes was able to combine gaiety in his conversation with seriousness in his work in a way that endeared him to his friends and mentors; when Francis Espinasse expressed his surprise that Lewes should be working on biographies of Robespierre and Goethe at the same time, Carlyle remarked genially that Lewes was not afraid of hard work. And when the *Leader* first appeared, not long after his own *Latter-Day Pamphlets,* Carlyle was suspicious of its socialism but referred to Lewes generously as the "Prince of Journalists."[22]

As his close association with Hunt, Mill, and Carlyle might indicate, Lewes moved in unconventional, perhaps even radical, circles. Later in life, he spoke of having suffered "the social persecution which embitters all departures from accepted creeds," an experience from which stemmed his "rebellious sympathy" with Spinoza, also an outcast. There is some romantic affectation in this remark; Lewes liked to talk of the necessity of suffering and experience for literary success, and some of the references to his own suffering are only poses. To be sure, Lockhart had written of Hunt in 1828 as "one who could touch nothing which mankind would wish to preserve, without polluting it," but the campaign of Lockhart and John Wilson against the Cockney School, though vicious and vigorous, hardly constituted social persecution. As for Hunt, Lewes himself argued in 1850 that although he was a "rebel in opinion, he has not placed himself at the barricades," and that while "some men intimate audacities parenthetically" Hunt always had a "parenthesis of propriety even in his most insurgent moods."[23] W.J. Fox's Chapel, though very much a part of radical London, was quite respectable. Some of Lewes' close friends in the early forties were perhaps less so: Thornton Hunt, Samuel Laurence, and John Gliddon seem to have been influenced by the moral libertarianism of Fourier and George Sand, and Lewes' close association with them has led some to claim that they had all lived together in a phalanstery. As Professor Gordon Haight has pointed out, the Leweses never lived with them; furthermore, the close relationship among the Gliddons, the Hunts, and the Laurences had reasons other than Fourier's law of passionate attraction: Gliddon was married to a Hunt, and both Hunt and Laurence were married to Gliddons.[24]

It cannot be denied that Lewes was intellectually daring and, at times, socially *outré;* these were functions of the irrepressibility of spirit that led Thackeray to remark that he would not be at all surprised to see Lewes ride down Piccadilly on a white elephant. His experience in green rooms and his readiness to discuss physiology and anatomy in polite company, in addition to his libertarian ideas, made his presence disturbing to his more conventional contemporaries. Mrs. Carlyle, however, found him highly amusing though one had to overlook his "unparalleled *impudence,* which is not impudence at all but man-of-genius *bonhomie.*" And, above all, she found no "spleen or envy" or any "*bad* thing" in him.[25] Nor were Lewes' associations all of the bohemian sort. In the mid-thirties—it would appear, even before his literary career had taken root—he discussed philosophy with a group that met in a tavern in Red Lion Square in London. It was there that he first heard the philosophy of Spinoza expounded, by a Jewish watchmaker of whom we know nothing other than that his last name was Kohn. This stimulated Lewes' interest in Spinoza, on whom he wrote a great deal and whose philosophy he regarded as the most internally consistent in metaphysical, as distinct from positive, terms. With William Henry Smith, a regular contributor to *Blackwood's* and his neighbor in Pembroke Square, Lewes spent much time talking about "lovely things that conquer death." He did not think much of Smith's metaphysical research, but felt that in literary matters they were at one.[26] Smith was instrumental in introducing Lewes to the publishers of *Blackwood's*, who began accepting his contributions in 1843. More than fifteen years later they began to publish George Eliot's works as well.

Through Leigh Hunt, Lewes met other literary or artistic young men, among them William Bell Scott. In a letter to Scott, Lewes revealed much of his own personality:

Sir—Leigh Hunt tells me that as "cordial natures" and as neighbours we ought to know each other. How far that is the case I know not, but this much I know, that we both agree in heartily loving Shelley, are fond of books, of poetry, — though you are a poet and I am none—. . . so in spite of its not being *selon les règles* of this most artificial of worlds, and might by most people be looked upon as impertinence . . . I take the shortest and easiest way I can think of for our better acquaintance. We are near neighbours. If we like each other we have only reached that liking *per saltum;* if we do not, why, no harm is done, we can "shrink into our conscious selves" once more.

During the thirties and early forties Lewes visited Scott often in his Hampstead studio, where they discussed various literary and artistic projects. But Scott felt somewhat threatened by Lewes' aggressive intellect. "Men who assimilate so quickly what is presented to them have a knack of using what they receive as if they had thought it out for themselves," he concluded. Thus, in the matter of the *Chorea Sancti Viti,* a project in which he proposed to describe the "stages in life of the self-seeking man of ordinary powers and unscrupulous ability," Scott felt that Lewes was about to "appropriate the idea in question, as well as all the others indicated in the designs, as his own, and to relegate" Scott himself to the position of an "illustrator."[27]

Yet another of Lewes' lesser-known associates, Stavros Dilberoglue, a Manchester merchant and friend of the Rossettis, appears to have inspired some of Lewes' more idealistic outpourings. To him Lewes addressed his open letter, "Communism as an Ideal," published in the *Leader*, in which he wrote of Communism as the necessary "consolatory faith." Furthermore, the character of Frangipolo in Lewes' third (unfinished) novel, "The Apprenticeship of Life," was said by Francis Espinasse, who knew them both, to have been based on Dilberoglue. If so, one might read something of the relationship between Lewes and Dilberoglue into that between Armand and Frangipolo, two characters in the novel, as though it were a palimpsest. In Frangipolo, "Plato lived again; but Plato Christianized—Plato shaping his course, not by a pursuit of the Graceful and the Good . . . but by the subordination of the Beautiful to Duty. The idea of Duty was his polar star." Under his influence, Armand, unlike most heroes in Victorian novels about intellectual and religious crisis, was converted from unbelief to faith. Lewes himself spent much time discussing the "redemption of Religion" with Thornton Hunt and R. H. "Orion" Horne in the late thirties. In the *Leader* he wrote another open letter, to David Masson: "Wherever the social theorist casts his sounding line he finds Religion: in Politics, in Morals, in Art, in Education, everywhere he finds Religion an Impulse or an Obstacle. . . . In the *Leader* more than one call has been made for the New Reformation,—or Church of the Future. . . . We want a new Church because the Church of

England, to all intents and purposes, is dead."[28] The flippant and French Mr. Lewes obviously had a serious core.

One of Lewes' older friends was Dr. Neil Arnott, who became George Eliot's "especial favorite." Arnott used to organize bachelor parties during which, for a while, the diners discussed Comte for Lewes' sake. Arthur Helps, later Sir Arthur, was especially close to Lewes, and visited him and Marian Evans in Weimar. He was one of the few to whom Lewes explained the whole story of his separation from Agnes and his living with Marian; later, Helps brought to them the news of the Queen's enjoyment of *Adam Bede* and *The Mill on the Floss;* and after his death in 1875, his daughter Alice frequently sought out the "Leweses" for company.[29] Lewes led an active social and intellectual life; his diaries and journals abound with references to the "good talk" or lack thereof at various gatherings. At the Museum Club, to which he introduced David Masson, he met George Smith, who had begun his proprietorship of Smith and Elder in the early forties, as well as Douglas Jerrold, Charles Knight, T. K. Hervey (of the *Athenaeum*), Thackeray, and various other publishers, literary men, and professional men. Masson remembered it as the "somewhat Bohemian resort of many wits and writers." It was there that George Smith made the acquaintance of the men who were later to contribute to his highly successful *Cornhill Magazine.* At the Fielding Club, so named by Thackeray, there was usually an "abundance of good talk," and sometimes "Vivian of the flowing locks" — Vivian was one of Lewes' pen-names in the *Leader* — might be found chatting with Charles Lamb Kenny in Burgundian *patois*, pretending to be French peasants discussing apocryphal wines.[30] Lewes would have been out of place at Clapham or Holland House or perhaps at the Athenaeum, but such was the variety of Victorian clubs —

the English answer to the French *salon*—that young and aspiring men of letters such as Lewes easily found congenial meeting places for their intellectual, professional, and social needs. Furthermore, Carlyle and Erasmus Darwin (older brother of the biologist) once calculated that there were no fewer than three thousand homes in London at whose dinner tables a man of any note would be welcome.[31] Lewes himself, when George Eliot had become famous and their relationship more acceptable (by the mid-1860's), entertained with great gusto. Of the Thursday dinners at the Priory where they made their home from 1863 onward, John Morley wrote: "I have never known such high perfection of social intercourse. . . . The guests were always the same, understood one another, spoke the same language, Spencer, Browning, Congreve, Theodore Martin, Harrison; talk of serious things without solemnity; nobody wanting to shine or to carry a point or to interject a last word; all kept in sympathetic play by Lewes's sparkling good humour."[32]

Like the theater, journalism was becoming respectable during the first half of the nineteenth century. Some of the milder abuses of an earlier generation were portrayed by Thackeray in his descriptions of the publishing houses of Bungay and Bacon in *Pendennis*. The profession had to live down a reputation for excessive concern for commercial success and indifference to truth or social propriety. Puffing of favored authors, savage criticism of those not so favored, sharp practices among competitors, and libelous scandalmongering—these were the bad old days. By the 1830's the influence of those like Leigh Hunt, Albany Fonblanque, Perry of the *Morning Chronicle,* Barnes of the *Times,* and Dilke of the *Athenaeum* established a tradition of integrity. At the same time, the social status of journalists improved considerably although there were persistent sneers such as

Le Machant's that "when Barnes lays down his pen he becomes a child." But if good society was not yet prepared to accept them, the journalists were becoming established as an essential part of the community as the rapidly growing demand for periodical literature testified. The middle class and lower-middle class required mediation between their understanding and the original minds of the age. Different periodicals responded differently to this need: R. H. Hutton's *Spectator* (1861-) was acknowledged to have broadened the minds of its readers but was considered "prosaic to the elect." On the other hand, the *Saturday Review* (1855-1938) was aptly dubbed the "Saturday Revilers" by John Bright; it claimed to speak for a university-bred class and was contemptuous of the general culture of the time. The *Leader* (1850-1860), which Lewes edited with Thornton Hunt, disdained merely to reflect opinion and saw itself introducing new issues "by offering free utterance to the most advanced opinions." George Holyoake, who was for a while its business manager and was quite advanced in his own views on free-thinking and cooperation, complained that the weekly was sometimes so progressive as to be incomprehensible to the average reader.[33]

In the late thirties, Lewes contributed a few short pieces to the *Monthly Repository* and a couple of minor magazines. His first major essay was "French Drama," published in the *Westminster Review* in 1840. Over the next few years he began to write for a widening circle of reviews, magazines, and serials: the *Penny Cyclopaedia*, the *Monthly Magazine*, the well-paying *British and Foreign Review*, the *Foreign Quarterly*, *Blackwood's*, and the *Edinburgh Review*, regarding which Lewes wrote: "a connection with it, however slight, would be too honourable for me not to be anxious to obtain it."[34] In the late forties, Lewes became involved in starting a weekly, the *Leader*, together with his friend Thornton Hunt, and Edmund R. Larken, a clergyman so liberal he appended to a volume of his sermons a sketch of Fourier's social ideas. It was necessary to make fund-raising tours and to find the right staff for the various aspects of magazine production. Thornton had had experience in editing and managing a periodical, but it was Lewes who supplied the enthusiasm. "D--n it, Thornton," he wrote from Manchester where he was trying to raise support, "the paper must be started. It is necessary for England and (what is more) indispensable to us! I am so sanguine of it that I would risk any money (would that I had it to risk) on its success."[35] Partly due to Lewes' driving energy, the *Leader* was launched in March, 1850. Lewes spent four years there, editing the literary columns and writing three or four pieces each week—book reviews, drama, criticism, and an occasional leader. During this period he also continued to write for other magazines and to do further research on Goethe.

To survey all that a single Victorian man of letters such as Lewes has written is a mind-numbing experience. The enormous variety of topics dealt with, the great number of books reviewed or alluded to, the seemingly endless prolixity of words, the verve and self-assurance with which each subject is attacked—one begins to wonder not only about the Victorian author but also about the Victorian reader. Such a being was omnivorous and insatiable; its demands for instruction were boundless, and its stamina equal to the stout volumes of reviews, monthlies, and magazines, not to mention the many-volumed works of fiction or general culture. To meet its demands the Victorian littérateur had to be able to write well and fully on many topics and often at short notice. Lewes' grounding at Dr. Burney's, his quick wit, his willingness to work, and his many journeys to the Continent enabled him to pick up new knowledge quickly, and it was this versatility which led to his success. The discerning assistant editor of the *Westminster Review* thought that he would do an article on modern novelists very well and also that Chapman ought to get him to write on Lamarck or some related subject for, "defective as his articles are, they are the best we can get *of the kind.*"[36] Lewes was aware of his facility and once received his comeuppance from Huxley. In a discussion on how difficult it was to write, he claimed boastfully that he never had any trouble working up the steam: "I boil at low temperatures," he said. "Ah," remarked Huxley, "that implies a vacuum in the upper regions."[37]

Many of Lewes' articles and practically all his plays were, indeed, potboilers; this was because the staggering variety of their interests made the Victorians, at their worst, cultural or intellectual magpies. On the whole, however, their concerns were solid and deep as well as varied, and in Lewes' work the impression of superficiality is more than offset by the seriousness and competence with which he dealt with French historiography, Spanish drama, Italian poetry, German philosophy, modern science, or individual literary figures. His attempts at poetry were disastrous, as painfully demonstrated by the following verse, written in 1843 but published only in 1850:

Gloomily sat Pontius Pilate,/Dark in gloomy thought sat he,
Sorely troubled in his spirit,/That he had not set Him free.
Many a quick and eager yearning,/(Roused by the Divine One's face)
Had been stifled by the clamours,/Of the accursed Jewish race.[38]

Lewes' novels were better, full of interesting details of literate, middle-class, urban life, but too full of heavy moralization and without sufficient genius for artistic or commercial success. *Ranthorpe* sold badly despite, perhaps because of, the fact the Lewes incorporated all his friends' criticisms; *Rose, Blanche, and Violet* did even worse though the author himself regarded it as a better novel. *The Apprenticeship of Life* was a *Bildungsroman* of far greater power than either and appeared serially in the *Leader*, but was never completed. In it Lewes' ability to depict characters and intellectual positions appears to have developed, though not yet the ability to sustain a coherent and convincing unfolding of the story. Nor did Lewes' early interest in drama lead to any original play-writing. He acted a little in the late forties, with Dickens' amateur group and — as Shylock — with professionals in *The Merchant of Venice*. But his acting, though competent, lacked forcefulness, and he contented himself after that with private, social performances.

As a drama critic, however, Lewes was quite successful: he was catholic in his taste, knowledgeable about all aspects of the theater, and "fun" as Shaw called it — "outrageously dressing up his laborious criticism" in a "recklessly flippant manner."[39] His *On Actors and the Art of Acting,* put together mainly from his pieces in the *Pall Mall Gazette,* is still considered a "greenroom classic." And many of his other pieces are still a delight to read; from them we get a better picture of Lewes' personal charm than from any of his other writings. His literary criticism was sometimes fussy in its pronouncements of general principles, but it was broad-minded — he championed Shelley and George Sand, and tried to correct the parochialism of English taste. His forte was an ability to "get up" an article on almost any subject. In addition to literature, Lewes had a deep interest in philosophy and science, and on these subjects Frederick Greenwood, the first editor of the *Pall Mall Gazette,* declared that Lewes could not be easily matched, "so versatile was he, so lucid, so sparkling and adept."[40] Sales of his *Biographical History of*

Philosophy (1845-1846) continued well into this century; in the 1930's Anna Kitchel found it difficult to get a second-hand copy, for, according to the dealers, the book was being bought up by university students. Francis Espinasse, who attended some of Lewes' lectures on philosophy in Manchester, thought that Lewes' listeners were most attracted by his contemptuous treatment of metaphysics: "It was pleasant to be told that though you had never troubled yourself about 'the problems of life and mind,' you were just as wise as any of the long series of sages who had wended their toilsome way on the 'high *priori'* road which, according to Lewes, led nowhere."[41]

Lewes was not satisfied, however, with merely passing on what he digested of other men's thought: he wanted to make original contributions of his own. In his exposition of Comte's philosophy of the sciences, for instance, he inserted discussions of the latest developments which had taken place since Comte wrote his *Cours*. Lewes' writings on science and philosophy are filled with suggestions for alternative theories and sometimes with jarringly self-important claims for his originality. Towards the end of his life, he attempted a grand assault on metaphysics in his *Problems of Life and Mind* (1874-1879). That he was considered by most of the reading public "merely a journalist and a critic," was as absurd, said Frederic Harrison, as if Bacon were to be known only by his *Essays* and Hume only by his *History of England*.[42] There was some truth in this extravagant praise from a loyal friend; nevertheless, it was the lightly carried learning of the *Biographical History of Philosophy* and the many articles on philosophy which established Lewes' reputation as a man of letters.

His first try at biography, *The Life of Maximilien Robespierre* (1849) — a hurried attempt to capitalize upon the interest aroused by the revolutions of 1848—was not a success but it has the merit of being one of the first to treat of Robespierre's career without hysteria. Lewes himself admitted in the preface that it was not a work of art or of "historical pretensions"—whatever these may be—but a "marshalling together of widely-scattered details, so selected as to present a view of the separate phases in the career of a remarkable man, and thus furnishing the data upon which a judgment of him may be formed." Lewes' second attempt at biography, on the other hand, was a capital success. *The Life and Works of Goethe* (1855) was a highly readable, perceptive, and comprehensive work. Into two medium-sized volumes Lewes managed to distil an impressive body of knowledge about and insight into Goethe's life and his many literary and scientific activities. Havelock Ellis was quite right in attributing Lewes' success with Goethe's biography to the fact that both men were "lovers of all things."[43] The several aspects of Goethe's life and work—poetry, drama, science—allowed Lewes to indulge his own restless intellectual curiosity, while Goethe's dominating personality gave the biography a unity which Lewes' other books lack. Practice at writing short pieces quickly tends to make more difficult the task of sustaining serious book-length treatments of a subject. In his famous lament on review writing, Walter Bagehot considered the defects of journalism to be that of "modern literature" as a whole—in variety, casualness, and impermanence. *The Life of Goethe* successfully overcame this occupational hazard of Victorian letters; it distinguishes Lewes' work from the mass of typical Victorian belles lettres, and it is still in print.

The mastery of the greatly divergent aspects of Goethe's life and interests which Lewes exhibited in *The Life of Goethe* seemed also to symbolize a new mastery over his own life and career. After years of experience in editing as well as writing, and with the history of philosophy and the *Goethe* both successful, Lewes "arrived" in 1855 as a talented, versatile, and hard-working man of letters. His career now came upon a clear turning-point; he did not abandon literature, much less philosophy, but he directed his efforts increasingly towards the study of natural science. And he established a household with Marian Evans. Both the change of interest and the decision to enter into an extra-legal relationship required great courage. It would have been easier to continue the exploration into literary and philosophic culture that he had performed with such gusto and occasional brilliance. But as some of his contemporaries punished themselves by climbing mountains, Lewes sought his mountain-climbing metaphorically and strove instead with craggy volumes of physiological lore. In 1855, he was ready to make science his major concern. For several years he searched for the boundaries between life and mind on the one hand and matter and material operations on the other, and pursued the scientific laws that would give certitude to some conception of life and of mind, of men and of things. This yearning for the positivist's grail led Lewes in 1867 to undertake a massive metaphysical project — to establish the foundations of a positivist (that is to say, empirical) conception of the universe that would satisfy man's need for a "meaningful 'cosmos.' "[44] This attempt to comprehend the universe, too, was characteristic of Lewes' age during which knowledge of the physical world, newly discovered or freshly asserted, appeared to subvert moral and religious — one might say, cosmological — tenets. Like George Eliot in her novels, Lewes tried, even more directly, in his philosophical writings to come to terms with both the new knowledge and the perennial need for cosmological "meaning." Even if his

solutions were somewhat idiosyncratic, his attempt embodied a typically Victorian concern.

Lewes' relationship with George Eliot has been well docu-
mented in Professor Haight's biography and magnificent
edition of her letters. Lewes had married Agnes Jervis on
February 18, 1841, and their marriage seemed to thrive on
the libertarian ideals and life-style of the circle in which they
moved. After a few years, however, the alert Mrs. Carlyle
noted that something was amiss. Lewes had returned from
his lecture trip to Manchester (March 1849) raving about
one Julia Paulet, her "dark luxurious eyes" and "smooth
firm" flesh; how had he known, his wife asked contemptu-
ously, which Jane Carlyle thought was the best way to take
"these things." In any case, she noted that the Leweses no
longer appeared such a perfect pair of love-birds.[45]

George Smith, who knew Lewes from the days of the Museum Club, remarked that he was fond of boasting of his
conquests and that he "preached a we-may-do-as-we-like
morality and, unless report maligned him, did very much as
he liked." Yet Lewes was no doubt sincere when he wrote:
"Home is like solid affection—we may be attracted from
both by gayer scenes and giddy flirtations, but we return to
them with redoubled pleasure." Lewes' relationship with
George Eliot was solid indeed, and Justin McCarthy remarked that the two phases of Lewes' character—from Vivian to editor of the *Fortnightly*—were like the difference between Prince Hal and Henry the Fifth.[46] Living with George
Eliot was not only an act of social courage, however, it was
also expensive. After the first year of his marriage, Lewes
managed to earn enough so that with Agnes' inheritance,
sale of stock, or the fee for a periodical contribution by
Agnes, their income was about £300 or more. According to

Mrs. Peel, gentility began with an annual income of £150; when Trollope married, he had £400 a year, which he considered "not very rich," although that was as much as the average beneficed clergyman might have, and a military officer would marry on less. To be comfortable in "good society" required £800 to £1000 a year.[47] The census of 1851 found the Leweses a comfortable middle-class household with two servants.[48] But when Lewes left with Marian for Weimar (July 1854) their financial future was not rosy. Of the £400 or so Lewes was now making each year, at least £250 had to go to Agnes and her household. George Eliot earned a little over £100 a year in 1854 and 1855. But for her eventual success as a novelist, their life together would have skirted the margin of gentility. Divorce, which would have been extremely difficult, became impossible after Lewes condoned Agnes' adultery and accepted her first child by Thornton Hunt as his own.

In Marian Evans, Lewes had a sympathetic and congenial companion; it was as though he found himself, after all the early years of bohemianism, in absolute devotion to the Sibyl of Mercia, whom "grave and wise men" credited with saving Victorian England single-handed, by her ethical teaching, "from the moral catastrophe which might have been expected to follow upon the waning of religious convictions." In time, Lewes began to develop what Professor Haight has called the "marmoreal image" of George Eliot. Others were infected: Oscar Browning reported that he was once greatly moved at the sight of George Eliot carving a leg of mutton with her "majestic arm," and that he regarded her as a prophetess—"her will to me was law, I enquired of her as of an oracle." Yet Lewes had the saving quality of not taking himself too seriously and retained something of his "unintellectual boisterousness" at their Sunday parties at the Priory; "who could help comparing the pair to Titania and Puck?"[49]

He took time, however, from managing her affairs with publishers and critics, and from handling her illnesses and acute diffidence, to edit various periodicals and to continue his research in philosophy and science. Walter Graham attributed to Lewes a large role in the success of the *Cornhill* and of the *Fortnightly*.[50] Darwin, it seems, proposed him for membership in the British Medical Association and the Linnaean Society and in 1876 Lewes became a founder-member of the Physiological Society. M.E. Grant-Duff reported that during a dinner conversation about Lewes, John Morley "put him very high as a philosopher, Huxley as a physiologist; Arnold thought him strongest as a dramatic critic."[51] It was a far cry from the days when Huxley attacked him for his "mere book-knowledge." In the seventies, the "Leweses" were accepted into many respectable circles. The career which appeared in the 1850's to have been jeopardized by momentous changes now gave promise in fact of having consolidated its success.

2 / The Man of Letters as Moralist

If, as has been suggested, the key word of the seventeenth century was "truth" and that of the eighteenth century "nature," then surely the key word of the nineteenth century was "morality." The great struggles for the abolition of slavery and for repeal of the Corn Laws were heavily charged with moral indignation; and at a different level, there was another battle going on, for civility and respectability against the harshness that had prevailed in the moral life of the eighteenth century. The resulting moral culture lends itself easily to caricature; the tendency to equate respectability with squeamishness and virtue with prudery, and the formalism, not to mention hypocrisy, of excessive concern for public opinion.[1] But there were profound reasons for the Victorian concern over morality. Many Victorians felt the moral life of man to be the last bastion against the onslaughts of rationalism. It was the "experience of moral obligation," Richard Hutton wrote in a critique of Feuerbach's "atheism," that "chiefly compels man to believe in a universal mental power distinct from himself and unfettered by limits of time and space." On the other hand, moral sensibility served also as the grounds on which many earnest Victorians like Darwin, Dickens, Thackeray, Francis Newman, J.A. Froude, and George Eliot felt obliged to abandon conventional religion.[2] Hutton and the believers might, through tortuous reasoning, come to hold that "in a sense, God is Himself, in all probability, no infrequent cause of the blindness of men to His presence." But Lewes was firm in the opinion that, as there was a punishment for not understanding God or His revelation, "obscurity is cruelty." He would reject out of hand any suggestion that the Fall might have been, paradoxically, fortunate. And he was particularly incensed at the Calvinist doctrine of the total depravity of man, calling it a "delirious drunkenness of theological pride" and a "blasphemy against the divinity [and] beneficence of God."[3] But if the religious view of men and things was not acceptable, what was to take its place? For Lewes and those like him it became an urgent matter to formulate and articulate a comprehensive view of art and society, and ultimately of the whole of the Victorian cosmos as well.

Lewes' criticism of society and of literature contained a strong, diffused moralistic core, which gave passion and at times a propelling eloquence to his writings. Sometimes this moral concern is not recognized as such, and appears disguised as some more intellectual consideration such as prudence or realism. On other occasions, Lewes consciously incorporated moral concern with intellectual analysis. At times morality appeared to be submerged under his main intellectual preoccupation—the reconciliation of empiricism and "philosophy." Unlike many of his contemporaries, Lewes was not content merely to offer ad hoc comments on particular works; he desired to comprehend each work with reference to the subject as a whole. His social criticism was full of reflections on the science of society, and his literary criticism of speculations on aesthetics. Nevertheless, in each area of thought moral considerations were deeply entrenched, sometimes distracting from the development of a coherent, truly original science of society or of literature. There were other reasons for that shortcoming: until 1855 Lewes had to make his living writing quick essays at more or less short notice; after 1855, his intellectual preoccupations were mainly scientific and philosophical. The combination, however, of moral concern, empiricism, and philosophic conceptualization made many of Lewes' pieces engaging and thought-provoking.

The Criticism of Society

"I am no politician," Lewes once wrote, correctly enough, for unlike Bagehot, John Stuart Mill, or Trollope, he neither cared nor understood nor wrote a great deal about the political issues of the day. What he wrote was mainly a result of moral outrage or abstract reasoning. He placed men of thought above men of action, because the latter were in his mind merely men of business, creatures of habit. Political leaders ought to be men of vision and conviction.[4] He meant not to preach abstention from action, however, but its subordination to reason; as one of the "young progressives" who had gathered around Leigh Hunt about 1837, as a follower of Mill and Carlyle, and as one who "agreed in heartily loving Shelley," he could hardly have been entirely apolitical. Among his early periodical contributions one finds, therefore, occasional statements of political principle and exhortations to civic virtue. It was Lewes, too, who pressed for the founding of the *Leader,* a weekly with advanced views, after Thornton Hunt seemed to have lost heart, and though Lewes was its literary editor, he occasionally wrote on public affairs as well. After he left the *Leader* in 1854, however, his interests shifted to science and he had even less time for poli-

tics. And though as editor of the *Fortnightly Review* he had
to give some attention to public affairs, it was only very
cursory; it was about this time that he wrote saying he was
"no politician."

In the late 1840's Lewes discovered, under the double inspiration of John Stuart Mill and Auguste Comte, the possibility of a science of society. His earlier writings on political
subjects had largely taken the form of vague condemnations
of social ills. The Comtist science of society gave clarity and
structure to his criticisms; but it also drew him into a number of awkward positions. It provided him with a useful slogan, "Order and Progress," with which to criticize the dis-
order of the left and the reaction of the right, which meant
that he had to wage a two-front battle. For him, the world
was both imperfect and in the process of getting better. He
would criticize the Tories for wishing to keep a grown-up
world in swaddling clothes, and he would chide a playwright
for exaggerating social conflict, asserting that the prejudices
of rank were "wonderfully . . . softened."[5] Further, Comte's
sociology, as a science, gave him a sense of certainty in his
political analysis. That very certainty brought with it over-
tones of determinism which conflicted with his instinctive
regard for individualism, diversity, and the moral responsibility of the individual. As a science, too, it necessitated an
abstraction and a generalization from facts which made it
somewhat suspect to the empiricist tradition in England.
Comte's science of society, however, claimed to be derived
from historical data and conceived of society as an organic
whole, thus enabling his analysis to ally itself with the Burkean strain in Victorian thinking. This conception of society
as an organism aroused Lewes' sympathies with the socialist
trends of the mid-century. At the same time, the idea that
society, indeed humanity, was developing and evolving

stirred some of his fears. Many of these tensions and contradictions, which are more or less universal in political theory,
remained implicit for Lewes. He himself did not seriously
attempt to think through the problems of political theory or
practice. Though his writings cannot be read as serious political analysis or theory, they tell us a good deal about the
political thinking of many Victorian intellectuals.

Very early in his career Lewes espoused the ideals of Shelley and asserted with fervor that Shelley's vision was proph-
ecy fulfilled. "Progression, humanity, perfectibility, civilization, democracy — call it what you will, this is the truth ut-
tered unceasingly by Shelley, and universally received by
us." Shelley was *the* poet for this new generation, Lewes
said, for he expressed its "collective creed" with "unyielding
worship of truth," undaunted by broadsides from the Tory
Quarterly Review.[6] Lewes realized, naturally, that the
Quarterly was representative of conventional wisdom, and
in April of 1847, he unleashed a bitter protest against the
voices of conformity: "let a man arise to utter the thought
which is struggling for utterance in the dumb million — let
him preach against a wrong which thousands feel. . . . Then
rises the voice of warning and of lamentation; then are the
lovers of social order called upon to repress the profligate
abuse of Liberty of Thought."[7] Order, Lewes asserted, was
only the shibboleth of foolish minds, for who denied its
necessity? Even radical criticism of society was concerned
with order, he said, pointing to Comte, the "most destructive philosopher of the present day, the one who would effect the most sweeping change in the present order of society
— who would introduce a new order growing up from a new
root."[8] New circumstances demanded not a return to the
ancient regime but an order which incorporated new situations — an order coupled with progress.

From an undifferentiated moral outrage, Lewes' sentiments appear to have developed into structured political
critique. The dogmas were lifted from Comte, the last volume of whose *Cours de philosophie positive* was a significant
attempt to construct a science of society. English liberals
and radicals, however, found Comte's analysis repugnant in
its authoritarianism. Thus, F. D. Maurice, a Broad-Churchman and Christian Socialist, was quick to see that positive
sociology was "conservatism in radical clothing," and
George Grote, a philosophical radical, refused to subscribe
to Comte's financial support for a second year.[9] On the
other hand, there were many who like Lewes appreciated
"the constant presence . . . of a vast meditative mind, earnestly aiming to unriddle the great mysteries of life, and to
make that life nobler by a wise subjection of the lower to the
higher impulses." What Lewes learned from Comte, in this
second phase of his political thought, included an articula-
tion of the preeminence of the intellectual life over the
material. The political and moral crisis of nineteenth-
century society resulted not from social contradictions and
class conflicts but from "l'anarchie intellectuelle." "What is
the *motor* of society," Lewes asked, "but opinion?" Those
who decry abstract speculation as remote and idle are as
ignorant and ungrateful as the sailor who sneers at the sublime science of astronomy.[10] The science of society would be
definitive and total; once established, there would be little
room for variety and no need for discussion. While this
authoritarian view of society might have appealed to a
generation which was in crisis and was seeking a way out of
the state of intellectual anarchy, it would deny whatever
liberal ideals that generation might have had.

The formula "Order and Progress" remained in Lewes'
vocabulary as a procrustean bed for his critique of English

politics. In his most extended political comment, a four-part article entitled "The Coming Reformation" (1847),[11] he argued with gross over-simplification that the Tories were overly concerned with the preservation of those institutions under which the nation had flourished. This was the surest way to guarantee revolution, for such old wineskins could not contain the ferment of the inevitable and continuous development of the nation. On the other hand, Tory institutions were better than none; he considered Owenism, Fourierism, and socialism to be "reckless and fallacious speculations." These radicals could offer only a destructive critique of society; their efforts at reconstruction were vitiated by the fact that they were advocating mere "paper constitutions." Their part in destroying the old forms of thought and old institutions of state and society was necessary, but they had no wisdom to impart regarding the construction of the new age.

As for the Whigs, Lewes declared that it was humiliating "to be forced to bestow our approbation upon a state of intellectual confusion, and to feel that it alone keeps us from a state of political tyranny or social disruption." He called Lord John Russell the "Duodecimo Statesman" and bemoaned the fact that "statesmen suited to its purpose every generation finds, / Hence our very little Johnny suits our very little minds." Like Carlyle, he missed the aristocratic will to power: "We object to vigorous Action: it would strain the nation's thews; / We object to all progression; we have calm and 'moderate' views."[12] The Whigs were the embodiment of that intellectual anarchy which was characteristic of an age of transition—what Lewes, borrowing Comte's language, describes as a transition from the military-monarchical-theological to the industrial-democratic-positive. Old ideas had lost their hold; old cosmologies had lost their

meaning. New ideas had not yet caught men's imagination.
A new coherent and comprehensive theory of society had to
be found; for a start Lewes recommended the study of
Comte's *Cours* and the sixth book of Mill's *System of Logic*.
"The Coming Reformation" cannot be taken as a serious
analysis of the political situation in England in the late
1840's. It shows little understanding of the divisions within
the various "parties," and its criticism of the parties was extremely conventional and overly schematic. What is interesting is that this analysis was wedded to an uncompromisingly
positivist view. Lewes followed Comte even to the extent of
advocating the suppression of private judgment. This must
have been hard for one who had only four months ago de-
nounced reactionary hysteria, but the infection of Comte's
concern for order proved momentarily stronger: "Convinced
as I am of the necessity for unanimity on all the great fundamental points — and this would still leave a large margin for
differences of opinion with respect to details — I see in the
principle of private judgment, so loudly extolled, a potent
source of anarchy, and I wish therefore to see it discredited,
but discredited solely by the excellence and truth of the
dominant opinions."[13]

It was not for nothing that his friend and colleague at the
Leader office, George Jacob Holyoake, called Lewes the
bravest man, intellectually, that he knew.[14] Once convinced
of the truth of a proposition, he was ready to accept it with
all its implications, though frequently out of enthusiasm
rather than on the basis of any critical evaluation. "The
Coming Reformation" was not, however, merely an instance
of Lewes boiling at a low temperature. It is true that never
again, despite a continual concern for order, did he so com-
pletely abandon the principle of freedom of thought, but
the intemperate outburst is a measure of the impact of

Comte's sociology. That science of society promised, at the same time, to be true to the existing realities and to elaborate comprehensively upon the laws governing society, thus providing certainty in social analysis; it would enable one to render a critique of society both empirical and philosophic, and to transcend the conventional dichotomy between natural and metaphysical or "national" and "philosophic" systems, such as Burke and Disraeli made. Like the doctrine of the hypostatic union, however, it was a highly intellectual and tenuous concept. In practice, the follower lapsed into one heresy or the other: either the empiricism and traditionalism of Burke or the pseudo-scientific authoritarianism of James Mill. Comte himself, because of his concern over "anarchy," was a pronounced authoritarian. For the moment Lewes endorsed such a position, but the Burkean tradition ran deep and strong in Victorian thought. Indeed, Lewes' enthusiasm over the incorporation of history as the basis for the science of society calls attention to the ambiguity of his position. For history was empirical and "national," and the science of society was abstract and universal.

History could serve, of course, as moral education and, like great literature, instruct by the extension of one's experience. The youth of England could, for instance, learn from the history of Rome, "*manliness* . . . so little cultivated in modern society," and would practise the difficult art of dispassionate analysis of political problems and solutions.[15] More than this, history was the "hieroglyphic monument of our past life," the decipherment of which would enable one to "understand the present and predict the future"; it was the "basis of social science—the foundation on which the gigantic superstructure of ethics and politics is to be raised."[16] It required, of course, a true philosophy of history to provide the true interpretation of the data, and such a philosophy was yet to be established, but Lewes was enthusiastic about the possibilities of Comte's "laws of human evolution," the famous *loi des trois états*.[17]

But, if history could indeed yield data for a social science, such a harvest might well prove an *embarras de richesse*. If, philosophically viewed, history could provide the verification of the laws of social statics and reveal the laws of social dynamics, it could also go further and demonstrate, more palpably, not the universality of these laws but a mind-numbing diversitarianism — to use Lovejoy's cumbersome but expressive word.[18] Burke had warned in the second preface to his *Vindication of Natural Society* that the study of society was a complicated matter, in which "we can never walk surely, but by being sensible of our blindness." Lewes, even in the 1840's, when he was most convinced of the validity of Comte's social pronouncements, wrote with great appreciation for the Burkean view of things. In his potboiling biography of Robespierre, published in 1849, he argued that it was impossible to single out the causes of the French Revolution or the measures that might have prevented it. In a way, this was the Burkean answer to the Burkean critique of the French Revolution — that the French Revolution was no less historically inevitable than the gradual development of the English constitution.

The main burden of Lewes' reflections was the complexity of history. Could anything so apparently ambiguous be a firm foundation for the science of society? The answer lay, it seems, in whether valid generalizations could be made in historical studies. J. S. Mill, the master of the Victorians who knew, thought that by calling in the "universal laws of human nature" to interpret history Comte had solved the problem, albeit with a methodological innovation. While in the physical sciences "specific experience commonly serves to verify laws arrived at by deduction, in sociology it is specific experience which suggests the laws, and deduction which verifies them." If sociological theory, arising as generalizations from historical evidence, contradicts "the established general laws of human nature," then the historical generalizations are invalid and the theory false. On the other hand, if such theory can be "affiliated to the known laws of human nature," if, that is to say, "the direction actually taken by the developments and changes of human society, can be seen to be such as the properties of man and of his dwelling-place made antecedently probable, the empirical generalizations are raised into positive laws, and Sociology becomes a science."[19] This reasoning is suspect, but for Mill the problem was not so much epistemological as moral: Book six of *The Science of Logic* began with a discussion of individual free-will in the context of historical and social generalizations with their determinist implications.[20] The epistemological problem was, however, present: Mill could not have forgotten Macaulay's devastating attack on his father's *Essay on Government*. Mill considered that Comte had solved this problem in the construction of a science of society by the emphasis on a historical, that is, an empirical, foundation, and thought this to be Comte's salient contribution to political theory. It made political theory less rationalistic and more authentic. Even so, it is doubtful whether Macaulay would have been reconciled to the argument from "universal laws of human nature."

Lewes seems to have understood these laws as being biologically rather than historically derived, thus avoiding the circular arguments. What he had in mind was not the argument from axioms regarding human nature that characterized Benthamite political theory but rather the derivation of social laws from biological ones as envisaged in Comte's hierarchy of the sciences. Even in Lewes' mind this does not reconcile the differences between the science of society and the relativity of history. On the one hand, Lewes asserted the possibility of sociology which required historical generalizations; on the other, he appreciated the complexity of history and doubted whether a science of society with laws of development was really possible.[21] Like many Victorian intellectuals, he sensed order and relation in the universe, but rejected the doctrinaire distortion of history to fit schematic outlines and the determinism implied in such schematizations. There was, however, one sweeping generalization that Lewes and most of his contemporaries found irresistible: that history was the demonstration of progress. In 1851 he wrote that the past revealed "that Humanity of whose life we partake — that vast chain of Existence which encompasseth us and all men, past, present, and to come, in one real vital brotherhood — a life which moves slowly, surely onwards, to grand predestined ends, without crushing or cramping the free will and energetic responsibility of each individual unit."[22] As J. B. Bury pointed out long ago the idea of progress, like that of Providence or personal immortality, cannot be proven or disproven. The passion and conviction that the notion of progress aroused can perhaps be best explained by seeing it as a kind of cosmology that met the needs created by the collapse of old philosophical and religious theories of the universe.[23]

Progress, however, was the optimistic face of the notion of development which, as Darwin thought, involved much waste and pain, and guaranteed no improvement. Constant evolution also subverted the absoluteness of moral or artistic judgments. And the idea of a gradual development had a strong conservative, as opposed to activist, bias. Neverthe-

less, for the Victorians, development meant progress. Lewes'
attack on Rousseau (1861) is a measure of this optimistic
faith. He was concerned solely with Rousseau's eulogy of the
"state of nature" and of the noble savage. The implication
that civilization was corruption and that thought and rationality contributed to degeneration rankled in Lewes'
mind. "No man having a soul," Lewes asserted, "can be
without a theory of life — a philosophy of some sort; . . . he is
compelled to speculate, and attempt an *explanation* of the
mysteries around him." As an attack on progress, Rousseau's writings were "at variance with all that psychology
and experience reveal." They ignored all history, which
Lewes thought had clearly demonstrated the triumph of
civilization. "Civilization therefore is indispensable to complete happiness: it excites greater wants, but in these very
wants there is activity, and man would rather have ungrati-
fied desires than be without desires at all."[24]

For Lewes and his generation, Macaulay's writings were
the complete embodiment of the idea of progress. Macaulay
was not philosophical, Lewes said, but he "unconsciously
submits to the influence of his age." He presented not more
antiquarian curiosities, but a thoroughly coherent and re-
assuring picture: the triumph of civilization and of moral
over animal tendencies. Even religion had progressed, for
men had become more moral and earnest.[25] It is true that
Lewes had some apprehensions regarding the philistinism of
material and social progress. There was, he noted regret-
fully, a tendency towards a "huckster morality" concomitant
with industrial and commercial development; and with economic growth there was over-indulgence, both material and
intellectual. Of Benjamin Frankin, Lewes said: "If the universe were nothing but a retail shop, Franklin was the man
to stand behind the counter — an exemplar of prudence, fru-

gality, honesty and independence. No mean virtues these,
but not the whole of our virtues — not our manhood."[26] But
these were more than compensated for by the "astonishing
progress in political knowledge, and in democratic views,"
and a "more thorough recognition of the rights of the nation
at large," he wrote in 1850, in a review of Harriet Martineau's *History of England during the Thirty Years' Peace.*
Philanthropy has become more practical, and there is now a
greater awareness of the need for "social justice." The progress of humanity would proceed past the era of landed
property and that of private property to that of humanity.
As an augury of that bright future, the thirty years of peace
had seen few great men; instead, the people had come to
center stage.[27]

In "The Coming Reformation" Lewes had dismissed socialism and radicalism as merely critical ideologies. By
1850, he recognized their constructive dimensions. The final
solutions to social and political inequities, he intimated,
would come from a serious consideration of Fourierism,
Chartism, socialism, and communism. In various statements
in the *Leader,* he was even more positive about these last two
ideologies.[28] One reason for this shift was that socialism, as
Lewes and many of his contemporaries saw it, meant an
organic, communitarian view of society as opposed to an
atomistic conglomerate, a *Gemeinschaft* as opposed to a
Gesellschaft. As such, this socialism could draw on the
sympathy among Victorian intellectuals for the German
romantic and French socialist conceptions of society, and on
their own Burkean tradition, which, though submerged
under liberalism and philosophic radicalism, surfaced from
time to time as in Lewes' reflections on history. And after
1848, as Halévy pointed out, far from being scared off by
the revolutions on the Continent, British public opinion,

through philanthropy or prudence, tended more and more
to take the view that revolutionary outbursts in England
were best prevented by raising the "moral level of these de-
graded masses," that is, by the intervention of the state in
their moral and physical welfare. Halévy noted, too, the influence of Mill's *Principles of Political Economy* (1848), the
second and third editions of which, appearing in 1849 and
1852, contained vigorous socialist arguments on property
and on the working classes, and the influence of Charles
Kingsley's Christian Socialism which made socialism respectable.[29]

The modification of Lewes' views was perhaps hastened
by the discussions and the canvassing in which he energeti-
cally engaged while he helped to found the *Leader*. His
efforts took him to Manchester and Leeds, and brought
him in contact with "advanced" thinkers and "socialists" like
W. E. Forster, G. J. Holyoake, Thomas Ballantyne, W. J.
Linton, J. A. Froude, and Edmund Larken. Forster was
then an advanced radical who advocated meeting the
Chartists halfway and who was a friend of Thomas Cooper,
the Chartist, and of Robert Owen. Holyoake was also a
friend, even a disciple, of Owen, and became the business
manager of the *Leader*. Ballantyne was an editor of the
Manchester Guardian and co-owner with Bright of the *Manchester Examiner;* Linton, the artist with republican beliefs,
found him the most congenial co-worker on the *Leader*.
Froude, whose *Nemesis of Faith* had recently been burned
at Exeter College, was a friend of Charles Kingsley. The
Rev. Edmund Larken, Lord Monson's brother-in-law, was a
Broad-Churchman with radical views and a willingness to
back them up with financial support. For Linton, the cause
of European republicanism was paramount, and he wished
to precipitate a similar movement in England. Thornton

Hunt and Lewes, on the other hand, seemed agreed on the
principle of free discussion of possible solutions to the social
and political problems of Victorian England. They wished
to provide an open forum for the uninhibited (but decorous)
airing of all opinions. A special section of the journal would
be set aside as an open forum. "In this arena the Tory or the
Communist, the High Churchman or the Low Churchman,
the Unitarian or the Sceptic may meet on strictly neutral
ground." This proposal of a free marketplace of ideas
disappointed committed radicals like Linton; it signaled a
retreat from Comtist authoritarianism and the reappear-
ance of a liberal concern for freedom of speech and discussion such as Mill was to immortalize in his *Essay on Liberty*
(1859).[30] The founders of the *Leader* wished also to preach
their own doctrines. Lewes was vague, but Hunt clearly
wanted it to support "full exercise of the franchise" for the
"whole people," secular education, complete and absolute
religious toleration, and free trade, and to foster "new
powers as the instruments for obtaining the fruits of opinion; *since opinion, without social influence and political
power, is a mere honorary and sterile distinction for the
community among which it exists.*"[31] On October 12, 1850,
Hunt, Holyoake, and Linton, with several others, formed
the National Charter and Social Reform Union in order to
try to unite Chartist, republican and reform groups. Like
other unions of its kind, however, it was a failure. Eighteen-
fifty was the beginning of more than a decade of political
complacency in England.

In the pages of the *Leader,* Lewes addressed himself to
the evils of competition. The inequities and miseries of
social life were not, in his mind, the results of the iron laws
of economics and production. They were the result of something intrinsic in human nature — the spirit of competition.

Like measles, it was not the more desirable for being practically unavoidable. To counteract the competitive spirit, the *Leader* kept its readers informed of the latest cooperative or associative schemes. And in its columns appeared a particularly passionate letter on that subject from Charles Kingsley: "I, as a Christian priest, do not deny the facts — for they stare me in the face. But, in the name of God I curse them, I declare them to be degrading, sinful, shameful; to be not human, but *inhuman and bestial.* . . . Brotherly help, not wolfish competition, is the ideal law, and shall be the actual state of men!"[32] As to what the future state, liberated from such bestiality, would be like, Lewes was cautious. He had not abandoned Comte's rigorous system of social laws only to take up another, less rigorous. "What shape is this new state to assume? . . . No meditative man will be ready to answer that: the answer rests with the future." Fourierism, Owenism, Chartism, and so forth were the "inarticulate utterance of some deeply-felt want." This reduction of the radical and socialist ideologies to their lowest common denominator denuded them of their concrete proposals for action, but Lewes was suspicious of panaceas. "Society," he said, "is a growth, not a transplantation."[33]

Furthermore, Lewes seems to have been vaguely aware of the dialectical nature of social change and of the unpredictability of the consequences of adopting "Communism." Some critics felt they knew what communism entailed and criticized it on grounds of its dangerous consequences. Lewes argued that to criticize existing conditions was one thing, to criticize a principle for its projected results was quite another. What Burke had made the ground for conservatism — the unpredictability of the chain of consequences following radical change — Lewes appropriated as an argument for toleration of such a change. In his literary columns in the *Leader,* he went out of his way to note every augury of the spirit of the coming age. "It is no longer possible," he wrote on May 4, 1850, "to 'pooh, pooh!' that which our philosophic publicists, our energetic clergy, our deepest-thinking dissenters, our wealthiest industrialists, and even our Tory organs, unite in declaring to be the grand question of the day." Many writers, indeed, Lewes claimed, had adopted as an alternative to competition the "principle of Common-work . . . which is the basis of all Communistic and Associative schemes." By this token, even "the greatest of modern political economists, John Stuart Mill, and several of the most distinguished members of the Church" could be included among the communists.[34]

This was no specter haunting Europe. Lewes described communism as advocacy not of violence but of cooperative ideals, not a program for action but a "consolatory faith, . . . an abstract conviction to sustain us while the grass grows." He would not even encourage radical social criticism. Forgetful of his own earlier scorn for "calm and moderate views," he rebuked Gerald Massey, a faithful contributor to the *Leader,* for the vehemence of his political poems. The "fierceness and rant" of these poems could, he conceded, be explained by the circumstances under which the poet grew up. Nevertheless, the poet "is doing hurt to himself and to the cause he espouses by allowing indignation to overwhelm truth."[35] Not all our geese are swans, Lewes said, and not all the swans of the enemy are geese. He was thus indulgent towards Bulwer-Lytton's aristocratic airs—"no one who calmly contemplates the influence of *race,* will sneer at such a source of satisfaction"—but cautioned him that history did not remember Bacon as Lord Verulam. Besides, the aristocracy of birth no longer exercised the power it once did. The "development of the industrial element"—which

Macaulay, for all the amplitude of his powers, had neglected to treat in his *History* — "has gradually destroyed feudalism; given birth to the true democratic spirit; and changed the whole constitution of society."[36]

Faith in the inevitability of social development inspired Marx to revolutionary praxis; it had the opposite effect on Lewes and most of his fellow Victorians because they believed also in the primacy of the intellectual, rather than material, source of social disorders. In a review of Sidney Smith's *The Mother Country . . . An Examination of the Condition of England,* Lewes declared: "We are at one with him when he says that people begin at the wrong end of Communism, taking hold of the tail of mere *material arrangement* before securing the head of moral adaptation."Among the many fallacies of Buckle's *History of Civilization in England,* he noted, "there is perhaps none so dangerous as his attempt to show the ineffectuality of moral causes in the advancement of civilization."[37] It was in order to further moral adaptation that Lewes and the *Leader* preached the virtues of debate and of education. And it was against Mrs. Grundy and the idols of respectability, whose influence tended to stifle free discussion, that Lewes unleashed some of his most vehement denunciations. In England, "a man may speak the thing he will," Tennyson had written; but, Lewes asked, *will* he? Truth may appeal to a man's intellect, but "he remembers that he is the father of a family, with sons to get established and daughters to get married — results not greatly facilitated by intellect, and seriously imperilled by his adoption of unpleasant truth.". The *Leader,* he complained in "Mrs. Grundy and the Public Press," had been advised to speak less boldly, to trim its sails, to sacrifice its convictions for the sake of respectability.

On the other hand, there were hopeful signals of the end

of Mrs. Grundy's reign. Francis Newman's rationalistic and highly controversial *Phases of Faith* appeared in the circulating libraries in June 1850, much to Lewes' pleasant surprise. "We cannot despair," he wrote, "when we know that such a spirit is abroad; when we know that earnest intellects . . . are becoming more and more alive to the importance of absolute freedom in discussion."[38] The *Leader* itself nobly championed that freedom by stoutly denouncing the anti-Catholic reaction to the reestablishment of the Roman Catholic hierarchy in England (November 1850). It was an unpopular thing to do, for nothing united the English people in the nineteenth century so much as anti-catholic feelings. Lewes himself had felt (in 1845) that Michelet, in his anti-clerical *Du Prêtre, de la femme, et de la famille,* fought against "an evil which we are all bound to take arms against, because it more or less openly menaces us all." The squire and the parson of Owen Chadwick's charming *Victorian Miniature,* High-Churchman and Evangelical respectively, were agreed on only one subject—that Puseyism should be "extirpated." And the working classes, as E.P. Thompson remarked, were always galvanized by the cry of "No Popery!" even if they did not know whether it referred to man or horse.[39] The challenge of Roman Catholicism ought to clear the ground, Lewes asserted, for its ultimate battle with the "Lutheran principle of the liberty of private judgment"—not in the halfway-house form the principle had taken in Protestantism, but in a new form emerging from the New Reformation. In this new form, religious concern would not be with the rightness of a creed, but with its uprightness, not with dogmatic but with moral truth, not with the form but with the sincerity of belief. This new form alone was the worthy counterpart of democracy in its struggle against absolutism. There was at least some pleasure in dealing with the Catholics: "they are logical, they are frank, they are explicit; with the slippery Protestants the case is not so easy to argue!" said Lewes. "Let the battle, then, be frankly fought between Science and the Church."[40]

The zest and eagerness for the combat to begin which Lewes displayed suggest a confidence in the outcome; he, at least, had no doubt that progressive elements would prevail. Here we note that contradiction, pointed out by Isaiah Berlin in his essay on Mill and the ends of life, of an optimistic faith in progress with the pessimistic premise built into the libertarian ideal of free discussion. The former implied a pre-determined end and the latter denied any assurance that truth could be found or would prevail over falsehood. Lewes too bore witness to the dilemma of liberal politics. But like Mill, he resisted the Carlylean temptation to "gag the fools, and establish the truth as a despotic Fact." Instead he waited for "Nature's laws to produce fruit in due time." Society was organic and "we must look to its culture, checking unwise impatience at the slowness of the growth."[41]

Slowness of growth, it may fairly be contended, is quite a different order of things from the inability of truth to establish itself. But the Victorian optimism had transmuted despair into impatience by the quiet hope that, though slow, progress would come, truth would out, and the grass would grow. Indeed, Lewes held some very complacent — and that is the opposite extreme of despair — views on intellectual innovation. He thought the "martyrdom" of Galileo to have been quite needless, and the publication of the *Dialogues* imprudent; Galileo should have published them as mathematical treatises, as he had been advised.[42] Thus Lewes affirmed his faith in the ultimate triumph of truth.

He appreciated but did not appropriate Spencer's analysis of evil as mal-adaptation; a situation about to be corrected by the process of development.[43] Spencer's analysis was neater, although Lewes too employed a biological analogy —society as an organism. That analogy was directly derived from Comte, of course, but was grafted onto the existing organic view of society which had been clearly enunciated by Burke and restated, for instance, in Tennyson's patriotic poems; and it modified the impulse to an "unyielding worship of truth." As a result, Lewes came close even to accepting slavery when he met with a plausible, Burkean argument for doing so in the Hon. Miss Amelia Murray's *Letters from the United States, Cuba and Canada* (*1856*). Slavery in the abstract was wrong, he declared; but could it in reality be abolished by legislation? "If all our abstract arguments are to be carried out into legislative acts, sad work will be made of the body politic," Lewes argued with characteristic British common sense: "Think of Socialist arguments! Think of the Republican axioms! Think of some of the simple maxims of Christianity, which are daily found to be impossible in our present condition!"[44]

This intellectualism, concern for order and progress, and Burkean vision of society can perhaps be seen as a reflection of middle-class concerns, but the concepts of interests and social classes are vague and controversial. In the Victorian case, economic lines are blurred by status considerations and confused by the remnants of a communitarian tradition which gave rise to such a significant phenomenon as Tory democracy. The usual tripartite division into aristocracy, middle-class, and working-class is practically indispensable in general discussion, but it does not seem sturdy or precise enough to bear an analysis of political alignment by classes. And yet a man's ideas would be eccentric indeed if they could not be related to concepts or attitudes generally held. Thus order and progress, in the Victorian context, might well be analyzed as a middle-class slogan in that it presents the ideal of order in confrontation with working-class agitation, and the ideal of progress as a challenge to aristocratic privilege. And there is, surely, hardly anything so transparently middle-class as Herbert Spencer's views on property: he attacked landed property and landlordism, typically aristocratic forms of wealth, and defended the typically middle-class form of wealth, private property, against any designs, radical or reactionary.[45] So to argue does not mean that one may make any causal connections between the social status of a man and his ideas. Shelley and Carlyle, both of whom influenced Lewes greatly, were two of the many writers who betrayed, if that is the word, their own class. The causal link is impossible to determine but the general comparison with the social and intellectual context adds a dimension to the understanding of a particular text or writer.

In the latter part of his career, as he became more established, Lewes' political ideas seemed also to become more conservative. But the changes and ambiguities of his politics are more easily attributable to the different influences bearing upon him at different times — Shelley's radicalism, Carlyle's moral outrage, Comte's rationalist science of society, Mill's liberalism, or the prevailing socialist winds in the middle of the century. Lewes' attitude towards democracy may be taken as an example. The early expressions of moral outrage and political concern can be mistaken as expressions of democratic sentiments; they were actually protests of liberal intellectuals against an aristocratic government; and the implications of their liberalism for the masses were not yet apparent. It was the people, meaning the middle class leading the (docile) masses, against the nobility. When the potential political dominance of the working class became gradually apparent to the intellectuals, there was much soul-searching, as is evident from the ambiguities in mid-Victorian democratic ideas. To put it crudely, advanced thinkers like Mill and Lewes were in favor of the broadening of freedom and political participation, but slowly. Thus, in the *Leader* and, to a less flamboyant extent, in the *Fortnightly,* Lewes and his colleagues aimed their analysis at those whom Holyoake called the "intellectual leaders of society" in order to liberalize their thinking, yet very few of the Victorian intellectuals actually did anything concrete for the political advancement of the working classes. Neither the teachings of Comte nor the example of English positivists persuaded Lewes to become involved in labor organizations.[46]

With remarkable foresight, however, Lewes appears to have recognized the wave of the political future; he noted that the most significant event of 1866 was the Congress of Working Men in Geneva. Indeed, he declared, only two other events in all of modern history compared with it: the rise of the communes in the twelfth century and the meeting of the Estates-general in 1789. And he sought to lead opinion to a calm and reasonable preparedness for the eventual dominance of the working classes, in much the same way as he earlier sought the establishment of the principle of cooperation — by incessant discussion of principles and examples, so that "by teaching and the *example of success* we may indoctrinate the nation, and make the change from old to new both gradual and complete."[47]

In the 1850's, Lewes defended the working class vigorously: they were good-natured and hearty, and became rascals only when in great want. Indeed, he argued, the wonder was that there was not more crime, considering the prevalence of poverty and ignorance. This idealization of the working class even entailed a radical defense of "stupid-

ity" which anticipated Bagehot's classic, conservative analysis of it. In an article on universal suffrage, Lewes replied to
the argument that the ignorant were not capable of choosing the wisest by declaring that what the state needed was
not a Frankfort "Parliament of professors" but "the great
qualities of manhood — energy, decision, honesty, fearless-
ness, and activity." These, he said, all men understood. As
"Vivian," Lewes drew a picture of an ideal citizen — "my
uncle Brown," simple as Felix Holt, and as sturdy: "He takes
in the *Leader,* for he is a sturdy Radical. He professes not to
make head or tail of our Socialism, and wants to know what
we are driving at: but he is a bold man, and is dreaded at
election meetings, where he 'speaks his mind,' strong in
sentiment though loose in syntax."[48] Lewes' idealization of
the working class was a somewhat maudlin attempt to assert
the essential goodness of the common man and thus to
persuade his middle- and upper-class betters that he was no
threat to them and that, given requisite education and a
cooperative society, he too could be a useful member of society. This was, above all, an appeal from a member of the
middle-class intelligentsia to his peers to extend the full
range of benefits and privileges of society to a hitherto
excluded class. And yet it cannot be denied that Lewes was
ambivalent towards democracy, towards the broadening of
political power and participation. According to Spencer,
"Reverence for humanity in the abstract seemed, in them
[Lewes and George Eliot], to go along with irreverence for it
in the concrete."[49]

Lewes' reservations, nevertheless, were not due to misan-
thropy so much as to certain serious defects which he thought
he detected in the idea of democracy. A fearful anticipation
of the worst consequences of democracy contributed to the
growing conservatism of Victorian liberals. Tocqueville and

Mill made their reservations known in the forties and fifties. The prospects of a "levelling" of society, whether political or cultural, appeared less acceptable as it became more imminent. As early as 1849, Lewes had criticized French attempts at democracy, on the ground that it was not the right principle for that nation. France must, he urged, "set aside the unreflective idolatry of democracy and . . . examine what are the real elements of French society" and proceed to frame a constitution accordingly. The gravamen of Lewes' argument was that democracy was unsuitable for France; its espousal violated, in effect, both Burkean principles and laws of the science of society. In 1851, he wrote agreeing with Guizot that democracy was "anarchical," that society needed a "higher guidance than that of any turbulent assembly, a higher faith than the faith in votes." Like Mill's, Lewes' defense of democracy was thus significantly qualified by a distrust of it. It was fortunate, he declared in 1856, that in the republic of letters "universal suffrage does not elect to the highest offices," and that "in science the vote of the majority is never asked."[50] Much as he sympathized with the cause of Italian unification and republicanism, he pleaded (in 1866) that Monte Casino, at least, should be spared the general fate of monasteries—conversion into barracks.[51]

Even during the period of Lewes' editorship of the *Leader,* his interests were beginning to range elsewhere. His preparations for the *Life of Goethe,* his trip to Weimar, and his subsequent engrossment in science, philosophy, and George Eliot left little time and energy for any sustained examination or reevaluation of his own political thinking. A decade or so later, when he declared himself apolitical, Lewes no longer thought of society as a subject for political analysis and criticism. Transmuted into the concept of "social medium," it became a matter for philosophic and scientific enquiry. Lewes explored neither the political nor the socio-logical implications of an organic view of society. Instead he was increasingly concerned with using the idea of a social medium as part of the naturalistic explanation of the intellectual and moral formation and activities of man. Moral indignation had sublimated into philosophic enquiry.

The Criticism of Literature

The Victorian concern for morality showed itself in litera-ture partly in the recurrent theme of moral crisis, which, not surprisingly, constituted an integral element in a great ma-jority of the crisis-of-faith novels. Furthermore, Victorian readers, as Hippolyte Taine remarked, seemed to instruct their novelists to be moral: "George Sand paints impassioned women; paint you for us good women. George Sand makes us desire to be in love; do you make us desire to be married." In response Anthony Trollope challenged the readers of his autobiography to search the works of the "six great English novelists" — Maria Edgeworth, Jane Austen, Sir Walter Scott, Thackeray, Dickens, and George Eliot — and see if they could find any element that would encourage moral laxity.[52] Criticism, too, was infected by this moral concern. Periodicals like the *Spectator* tended to view art as a branch of moral philosophy, and critics like Leslie Stephen or even Arnold were imbued with a strong sense of what ought or ought not to be written with a view to improving the moral climate. Lewes' criticism was often highly moralistic despite vigorous pronouncements against "the cant which perpetu-ally demands 'the moral' of a work of art." The criterion, he said, should be not morality but truth. He therefore cham-pioned the works of George Sand, and in the preface to *Rose, Blanche, and Violet,* he stated that "the Moral has been left to shift for itself. It was a choice between truth of passion and character, on the one hand, and on the other, didactic clearness. I could not hesitate in choosing the former."[53]

In practice, however, he could not help using morality as a criterion. In a comparison of George Sand and Balzac, he declared that there were three "points of view" for judging a novelist — as moralist, as artist, and as entertainer. And he argued that George Sand was the superior moralist, for, unlike Balzac, who was flippant about marriage and adultery, she was not; "she has never made adultery a jest; always a crime terrible in its Consequences." Even so, some of her perceptions into life troubled him; because her truth was often hideous and painful, he found himself declaring that, though a novelist must write out of experience, a discrimination had to be made between "the legitimate and illegitimate employment of experience." Lewes conceded that art could not "prove" morality, but he argued that it could *show,* and could thus mold moral sense by reinforcing "truth long since ratified by our consciences." He was probably expressing the sentiments of a typical Victorian when he said that, if the villain of a piece got away with his mischief, he would feel "Oh! I wish I could punish that fellow." And despite what he said in the preface to *Rose, Blanche, and Violet,* that novel itself was a dreary tale of truth and consequences. He deplored the "sickly sentimentality" of the circulating library, of course, and he praised Mrs. Gaskell's *Ruth* for its "strong" views. But for him the "strength" of these views lay in the clear distinctions it made between right and wrong. Charlotte Brontë's *Shirley,* therefore, displeased him, for it presented the two "heroes" as having "something sordid in their minds, and repulsive in their demeanour."[54] Such moral ambivalence might be allowed in minor characters, but not in the heroes of a novel.

Much of Lewes' concern was provoked by the proliferation in his time of literature in general and of novel-writing in particular: when "it became possible for an author to earn by his pen an honorable livelihood," he complained, "the *trade* of literature began." And the sketchy and frothy products of this trade debased the "taste of the age." He did not believe that this great evil could be corrected by an Academy or any external authority; he appealed instead to the "self-respect" of the men of letters, and asked that critics take upon themselves the task of watching over the literary productions of their day. The English people, Lewes claimed, were moralistic, indeed they were prudish, but they needed to have the object of their moral indignation pointed out to them. Thus he warned his readers against the danger of "great injury" to their taste in the lurid sensationalism of Eugène Sue, and praised *La Tulipe noire* as a work which "the most fastidious parent can place without a moment's hesitation in her daughter's hands!"[55]

In an important article published in 1865, Lewes acknowledged that the good that could be effected by such criticism was little; on the other hand, the danger was everpresent that fear of vigorous criticism might restrain originality and individuality. That danger existed because "critical standards [were] being almost universally formed not according to what is eternally true and necessarily pleasing, but according to what has already pleased, and which is precipitately generalised as alone capable of pleasing." This was an intimation of the awareness that new works might necessitate a change, a development perhaps, in critical standards; the principle of critical flexibility, which he had

learned from the Germans, had to be applied when dealing
with individual works as well as with foreign literature.
Critics ought, therefore, to eschew hasty and pontifical
judgment, and admit that their criticism reflected their
personal opinions, and no more, until the discovery and
formulation of "certain psychological principles to which all
works must conform, and certain technical principles by
which every art must be guided." When a critic judged by
these universal and eternal principles, his judgment would
be "true of all minds and at all times."[56] Critical diffidence,
even subjectivity, was to be a temporary measure until a
science of criticism emerged which would deal with individual works from a universal point of view.

Great art, Lewes declared, must appeal to all ages and to
all nations; for art "deals with the broad principles of
human nature, not with idiosyncrasies." The laws of the
construction of a novel could be compared to the law of col-
ors, as they were "derived from the invariable relation between a certain order and succession of events, and the
amount of interest excited by that order."[57] Lewes formu-
lated his first extensive plea for a literary theory in "Hegel's
Aesthetics: Philosophy of Art" (1842). He devoted a large
part of his commentary to Hegel's definition of poetry as (a)
the metrical utterance of emotion, and (b) the "beautiful
phasis of a religious idea"; that is, the definition of poetry
as the expression of one man's feelings is also, in some
measure, the "formula of any truth leading to new contem-
plations of the infinite or to new forms in our social relations." The central meaning of these strange phrases — that
literature was not only the creation of one man but also the
expression of the intellectual life of the nation — remained a
"fixed idea" for him. Moreover, Hegel's *Aesthetics* provided
Lewes with the occasion for a comparison of the state of crit-

icism in England, France, and Germany. Whereas critics on
the Continent had a vision, a point of view, and ascertained
principles, criticism in England, he said, tossed on a "great
ocean of uncertainty, on all points deeper than mere
technic."[58]

Against the typically English opinions that criticism was
cold, that rules cramped genius, and above all, that Shakespeare had known "little Latin and less Greek," Lewes tried
to argue that Shakespeare had been " 'wise in all the wisdom
of his time,' " and that the times had changed so that, even
if it had once been true that art flourished without criticism,
the present age was "more critical and conscious." Criticism
was necessary so that a poet might have a "sympathizing,
reverent and affectionate sister, who will assiduously fetch
out the latent meaning, and irradiate, with her understanding, those more dim and intense feelings of his imagination
which may have found expression in unusual forms." Such
criticism would have to be philosophical, that is, based upon
an aesthetic, for "criticism is to æsthetics what the practice
of medicine is to physiology" — the application of knowledge
of the general to particular cases. Such philosophical criticism, such a "Sinn für ein æsthetiches Ganzes," was, unfor-
tunately, hardly to be found in England. In Germany, however, criticism enjoyed the firm foundation of well-articu-
lated æsthetics, such as Hegel's; Lewes commended it to the
study of his readers, but warned that those who were not in
earnest should keep away from it, for they would find it a
closed book and would only "rise from its non-perusal to
gabble about its 'German mysticism.' "

There is no need to belabor the contradiction between
this appreciation of philosophical criticism and the dispar-
agement of it found elsewhere in Lewes' work. It was in part
due to the occupational hazards of Victorian journalism.

More significant was the realization that the philosophical
nature of such criticism did not safeguard it from absurdity.
Lewes dismissed A. W. Schlegel, who had the bad taste to
consider Calderon superior to Shakespeare, as someone who
passed off "easy theorizing for philosophic judgment." And
he criticized Hegel for his attempt to argue that Goethe's
Hermann und Dorothea was more German than Voss's
Luise because, in the former, Rhine wine was served instead
of coffee, as in the latter. Lewes argued that in Voss's story,
where the setting was a parsonage, the common drink was
coffee; the characters of *Hermann und Dorothea* drank
Rhine wine because they lived in the Rhineland: "To such
prosaisms is the British critic reduced in answering the sub-
tleties of German aesthetics," he declared with an air of triumph.[59] Indeed, much as Lewes appreciated the notion that
philosophical aesthetics guided practical criticism, he also
found much to scoff at in German literature and criticism.
In 1845 he warned against the dangers of excess in the current predilection for German literature as a whole; quoting
Burke on moral masquerades, he argued that literary imitations resulted in the loss of one's literary nationality without
the gaining of another. A little exposure to foreign literature
was necessary for broadening the mind, but too much could
result in the unconscious adoption of new prejudices. The
one German, apart from Goethe, to be allowed through
this literary cordon sanitaire was the "eminently British"
Lessing, whose work was entirely free from *Schwärmerei,* "a
word untranslatable, because the thing itself is un-English."
His writings, unlike German literature in general, did not
lack "distinct purpose," "masculine character," or a "chas-
tened style."[60]

It should be noted that Lewes did not reflect upon the
aesthetic work of either Hegel or Lessing as a whole. There is

no sense of awareness in his article on Hegel of what Wellek described as the carefully balanced and closely reasoned treatment of the relation between thought and reality, content and form. Nor does he manifest any appreciation for Lessing's brilliant synthesis of Enlightenment wisdom, as Cassirer put it, on the resolution of the conflict in art between "generality" and "definiteness."[61] Lewes merely appropriated from one the idea of philosophical criticism and used the other as the springboard for a discussion of muscular common sense in literature. Nevertheless, if his remarks on Ruskin are any indication, Lewes still desired to see English criticism become more "organized" and philosophic. Ruskin's *Modern Painters,* he said, "furnished another example of the old truth, that empiricism is as idle and pernicious in Art as in Philosophy, and that only by the recurrence to those eternal principles from which Art itself issues can criticism hope to utter a sane word."[62] Lewes was quite vague as to what these eternal principles were; we can only surmise that he rejoiced over Ruskin's vision of art as "the great humanizing activity and achievement of man" a vision in complete contrast to both the philistine utilitarianism of his age and the amorality of the "art for art's sake" school of thought. Lewes translated this vision into the principles of vision, sincerity, and beauty in the most sustained piece of "literary theory" that he wrote, "The Principles of Success in Literature" (1865).[63] Ruskin's views on the organicism of art and society and on the identification of art and morality fell, of course, on prepared ground, and his revulsion against Germanic terminology surely struck a sympathetic chord in Lewes' mind.

Like his treatment of philosophical criticism, Lewes' attitudes towards romanticism and classicism were ambivalent. Romanticism was a necessary reaction to the conventionalism of classicism, but he could not condone its luridness and perversity. He conceded that Victor Hugo had "high aims and splendid talents," but complained that in the prolixity of language and imagery there appeared "little respect for truth" or "solicitude about sense." The self-appointed literary taster for the Victorians turned with relief, he said, from the "convulsive school," which included Balzac, Dumas, and Eugène Sue, to the insipid dramatic works of Latour de Saint-Ybars and François Ponsard and to George Sand—not only for the moral earnestness of her works but also because her style was in the great tradition of Racine, Bossuet, Voltaire, and Rousseau.[64] In a letter to Macvey Napier (in 1843) proposing an article on Boileau for the *Edinburgh,* Lewes argued that "in these days of false taste and vicious writing" it was necessary to hold up the "excellent good sense" of Boileau. It is clear that Lewes only wished to use the classical school as a moral antidote to certain poisonous tendencies in Victorian literature; he had no desire to adopt classicism as a literary theory. For in his mind, which was not entirely settled on this matter, the classical school had repressed "all originality and all progress." English poetry, like English gardens, when compared to their French counterparts, displayed "a closer imitation of nature, with a greater disregard for mere technical excellencies."[65]

As with the science of society, aesthetic theory required a resolution of the tension between empiricism and abstraction. In art, where great genius was distinguished by the concreteness of its vision and imagery, how could one forge a science of the "eternally true and necessarily pleasing"? In his attempt to articulate an empirical aesthetics, two concepts predominate: that of realism, or truth of vision, or authenticity, and that of success. Art, Lewes wrote in 1858, always aimed at the "representation of Reality," that is, of truth. "Realism is thus the basis of all Art, and its antithesis is not Idealism, but Falsism." Authors might choose different subjects, adopt a diversity of points of view, and treat their subjects with varying sympathy, but their writing must be *true*. At one point, he asserted that "the true Realism of art consists in representing common objects and common experience with lovingness as well as truthfulness." But Lewes placed greater emphasis on his criticism on the discrimination between realism and "detailism" or "waist coat realism." Artists had become photographers, he complained in "Principles," and "have turned the camera upon the vulgarities of life, instead of representing the most impassioned movements of life." He condemned this sort of realism as symptomatic of a "creeping timidity of invention." Art should "stir our deeper emotions by the contagion of great ideas," and should therefore reflect that which made life "noble and solemn." Lewes deplored the fact that realism, as practised in the mid-nineteenth century, tended to trivialize art and life by the prolixity of the details it furnished when untempered by any sensible, artistic selection; it was, he declared, in the *"selection of the characteristic details that the artistic power is manifested."*[66]

Lewes was concerned, in drama as well as in art in general, that naturalism, or realism not be confounded with the depiction solely of the trivial or "vulgar" aspects of life; naturalism must extend to the portrayal of the heroic as well as to that of the vulgar, of Achilles as well as of Thersites. And although acting ought to be realistic—"natural," a "truthful presentation of the character indicated by the author"—the conditions of the stage required a modification of realism. Indeed, one of the distinctive aspects of art in this medium was that it demanded from its audience the "alchemy" of imagination, and attempted naturalism such as the placing of real trees on stage was incongruent with his art form; it substituted for that "alchemy" a very "prosaic positive chemistry."[67] Not surprisingly, Lewes did not try to elaborate a psychology of spectatorship.

Of a different literary genre, Lewes went back to the positivistic view, prosaic though it was. Historical romances, he declared, were difficult to write well, although after the success of Sir Walter Scott there had been a flood of pseudo-historical romances. The paucity of established facts could only foster inaccuracy in historical novels and dramas: "If we are ignorant, we are fearfully misled," he said; "if we are instructed, we are unpleasantly disturbed by the falsifications and errors." Scott had "damaged the study of history" by casting it as a source of entertainment and thus leading other writers to emulate his "picturesque effects" rather than to attempt to teach history. And he dismissed Alexandre Dumas' romances as "not historical but hysterical."[68] These *obiter dicta* merely show how easily the ideal of truth or literary authenticity could be debased into an obsession for factual accuracy.

In *The Life and Works of Goethe* (1855), however, passages of considered literary judgment are interwoven with reflections on the relationship between art and politics, on the nature of scientific activity from a humanistic point of view, and on morality. In 1843 Lewes had published an article, "The Character and Works of Goethe," pompously declining to view Goethe as either a charlatan or a "Weimarian Jove, sitting high above this imperfect world, smiling serenely, contemplating its short-comings with pity." Instead, he proposed to analyze Goethe's character, in particular his reputation for "coldness," which Lewes attributed to the "intense susceptibility of his nerves to all impressions." Goethe kept aloof from religion and politics, and even from occasions of violent grief or passion, in order to preserve his artistic sensibilities and detachment. This great sacrifice to art, like Fichte's devotion to philosophy, resulted in a truncation of his personality. Neither man, Lewes declared, realized that religion, philosophy, and art constituted an "indissoluble trinity; but each separated his favorite element and proclaimed that to be the whole."[69]

In his book-length biography, Lewes presented a sympathetic and appreciative picture of Goethe's many-sided ability, interests, and life. He did explain Goethe's "political indifference" with a reference to his "earnestness in Art" which he said, perhaps by way of oblique self-correction, "has been made the evidence of this most extrordinary charge against him, namely, that he 'looked on life only as an Artist.'" But Lewes argued this time that art enjoyed the "serious privilege" of drawing away a man's thought and activities from other "great pursuits." And he did not attribute to "want of moral enthusiasm"—a phrase he had used in "Character and Works"—the absence of moral verdict in Goethe's work; rather, he vigorously defended it as moral realism. Like Shakespeare, Goethe was a "decided realist." Each was content "to let his own pictures of life carry their own moral with them." The scenes depicted in *Wilhelm Meister* were familiar to everyone except children, and if any reader could be "morally injured" by the reading of such scenes, Lewes said, "his moral constitution is so alarmingly delicate and so susceptible of injury, that he is truly pitiable."[70]

The realism of Goethe's approach to moral situations pervaded the other aspects of his works. Borrowing an epigram from Friedrich Schlegel, Lewes declared that every man was either a Platonist or an Aristotelian, his intellectual

bent either subjective or objective, his view of things either
ideal or concrete. Goethe, he said firmly, was an Aristotelian: "In every page of his works may be read a strong feeling
for the real, the concrete, the living, and a repugnance as
strong for the vague, the abstract, or the super-sensuous."
In the third edition of his *Life of Goethe,* Lewes added a
passage to make explicit the parallel between the opposition
of the realistic to the idealistic, and that of the positivist to
the metaphysical: "The achievements of modern Science,
and the masterpieces of Art, prove that the grandest generalizations and the most elevated types can only be reached by
the former [Aristotelian, realistic, positive] method; and that
what is called the 'ideal school,' so far from having the
superiority which it claims, is only more lofty in its pretensions, the realist, with more modest pretensions, achieves
loftier results."[71] Lewes thus contradicted what he understood as Goethe's "synthetic" attitude in science; indeed, he
had suggested that it was Schiller who influenced Goethe to
be "speculative and theoretical, in contradiction to his
native tendency." The contradiction is symptomatic of
Lewes' difficulties with the divergent claims of the concrete
and the universal; it is made slightly less glaring by Lewes'
explanation that hypotheses could be justified by rigorous
verification, and that in Goethe, "as in the men of positive
science, an imperious desire for reality controlled the errant
facility of imagination."[72]

Goethe's science was, therefore, an empiricism with
soul-satisfying "ideal construction," and his art, a realism of
solemnness and nobility. *Hermann und Dorothea,* though
the "most truthful" of all poems describing country life and
country people, was at the same time a clear, even epic, reflection of universal human experience. *Wilhelm Meister*
provided Lewes with the occasion not only to state his views

on "moral realism," but also to pour scorn upon philosophical criticism." The German critics of this school, he said, translated art into philosophy and called it philosophy of art; they were as afraid of the "surface" of literary works as they were of cold water, and therefore bored into literature for the Idea or Meaning. By way of corrective example, Lewes proposed to subject *Wilhelm Meister* to "historical criticism," in the course of which he established the fact that the first six books were written before Goethe's Italian trip, while he was full of delight in his role as manager, poet, and actor, and related the "healthy objective facts" of dramatic life. The final four books were written ten years later, when, realizing the futility of his attempts to create by nurture what he lacked by nature, that is, dramatic ability, Goethe conceived the idea of making his story a symbol of the "vanity of cultivating an imperfect talent." The first portion was clear, healthy, unpremeditated; the second was over-burdened with symbolism and Meaning. One dealt with life, the other with abstractions.[73]

In his chapter on the first part of *Faust,* Lewes declared: "In studying a work of Art I proceed as in studying a work of Nature: after delighting in the effect, I try to ascertain what are the *means* by which the effect is produced, and not at all what is the Idea lying behind the means." The understanding of art, he wrote in a different context, came only through the patient examination of a "large observation of successful efforts" and the deduction of "general conclusions respecting the laws upon which success depends."[74] Goethe's *Faust* succeeded immensely; its popularity ranked with that of *Hamlet.* And Lewes found the reasons to be similar: apart from providing a "prodigality" in the representation of the many different aspects of life, both plays also depicted what he rather vaguely referred to as "the eternal problem of our intellectual existence." The dullest soul, Lewes declared, "can *feel* a grandeur which it cannot *understand,* and will listen with hushed awe to the out-pourings of a great meditative mind obstinately questioning fate." It is not entirely clear if the "eternal problem" Lewes had in mind was what he then described as the spirit of the Faust legend. This spirit, he declared, had remained unchanged; it led to the "sacrifice of the future to the present . . . . the blindness to consequences caused by the imperiousness of desire," and the reckless endurance of consequences, provided a temporary pleasure could be obtained. It was this, he said, "which dictated Faust's barter of his soul, which daily dictates the barter of men's souls."[75]

This intellectual and moral—indeed, religious—aspect of *Faust,* wedded to a luxuriant presentation of life, was the source of its success. Geniuses, Lewes said, could find "materials in the trifles ordinary minds pass heedlessly by," but only a combination of a great mind with a great subject would produce an outstanding work of art.[76] To say that great success arose from the efforts of great genius upon a great subject does not, however, add anything to our understanding of literary success, let alone of literary values. Lewes' remarks on Goethe's works have an attractive directness and, often, an air of plausibility about them, but they do not add up to any literary theory. The avowal of critical realism, or Aristotelianism was all very well; it did not lead to a systematic, scientific aesthetics.

In "The Principles of Success in Literature," Lewes made the most extended of his attempts to articulate a comprehensive, coherent, and scientific view of literature. He began with an arresting comparison of the place of literature in society with that of the nervous system in animal organisms. The more developed the animal, the more "imperial" the character of the nervous system. Similarly, "as the life of nations becomes more complex, thought assumes a more imperial character; and Literature, in its widest sense, becomes a delicate index of social evolution." During the early Victorian years, the production and readership of literature had mushroomed. To Lewes, this was a sign of the passing of the last remnants of the feudal age; the pen, he said, now counted for more in society than even the feudal sword. But the emergence of "mass culture" and of professionalism in literature also made it imperative, he thought, to encourage good literature and to discourage bad literature. To this end, Lewes proposed to examine the factors involved in good literature, which he equated with what succeeded. "Success is not an accident," he said. "All literature is founded upon psychological laws and involves principles which are true for all peoples and for all times." And, as a testimony to the strength of his moral concern, he did not fail to add that no talent could be "supremely effective unless it act in close alliance with certain moral qualities."[77] The principles of success in literature were, according to Lewes, Vision, which was intellectual; Sincerity, which was moral; and Beauty, which was aesthetic. The three might be considered different aspects of one principle, and indeed they overlapped in their spheres of operation.

All good literature rested on insight, that is, on vision, which had to be "authentic," derived from the artist's own experience. Obviously, only a very few could truly *see:* others were refiners of the ore; and then there were the masses of imitators and compilers, mere echoes and echoes of echoes. Lewes was sternly opposed to those who wrote with borrowed insight—"seeing at second-hand" he called it—and he condemned it in tones both moralistic and positivistic. "Every sincere man," he said, "can determine for himself whether he has any authentic tidings to communicate," and he should not communicate anything he had not personally "verified." Vision and discovery, the act of artistic creation and the process of scientific conceptualization, were similar mental activities. "The discoverer and the poet are inventors," he said, "and they are so because their mental vision detects the unapparent, unsuspected facts, almost as vividly as ocular vision rests on the apparent and familiar." Vision, of course, did not necessarily mean the imagination of the extraordinary, of the spectacular or the heroic; it was just as difficult (and valuable) to have fresh insight into the ordinary. Indeed, Lewes said, "the imagination is most taxed when it has to paint pictures which shall withstand the silent criticism of general experience"; such was the artistry of Jane Austen. And Scott was not more extended in writing about Saladin and Richard Coeur de Lion than he was in describing the Mucklebackits.[78] If a man's vision was of the fantastic—of angels or demons, pixies or mermaids, a hippogriff or a centaur—it had nevertheless to be authentically present in his mind's eye; Lewes was unwilling, however, to allow imagination to run riot (as did Victor Hugo's); he required that vision to "correspond with our sense of congruity"; no appeal to insight or vision or even poetic licence could justify a statement that moonlight *burnt* a river bank. Like "ideal construction" in science or philosophy, imagination must be verifiable, that is, relatable to experience. "Unless a novel be built out of real experience," Lewes cautioned the author of *Jane Eyre,* "it can have no real success."[79]

Most characteristic and revealing of this notion of vision was Lewes' enthusiastic review (1861) of John Petherick's *Egypt, the Soudan, and Central Africa.* The book, Lewes explained, was the "cream of sixteen years' experience," and was "straightforward, pertinent, brief, unaffected" — like its author, whom he described as "a man without sham sentiment, sham enthusiasm, sham beliefs — a man with an open eye, a strong hand, a good digestion, a happy temper — not without a spice of the devil at times — and rare self-command . . . the very man to subdue savages by a mingled audacity and prudence."[80] In other words, he was the very wish-fulfilment of Victorian masculinity. Despite this outburst of unabashed Englishness, Lewes' literary sensibilities were sympathetic to other visions and experience as well. He praised Leopardi as a "poet of despair" without peer. His works bore the stamp of authenticity; they came out of intense experience, and Lewes' only complaint was that this experience was not sufficiently extensive. Lewes even argued that Alfieri's plays, filled as they were with a Shakespearean vehemence and subtlety of passion, justified the "moral failures" that marred Alfieri's life.[81] The demand for authenticity of vision was apparently strong enough, at times, to overcome Lewes' moral qualms.

No less insistent were Lewes' statements regarding the necessity of sincerity, the moral aspect of the principles of success.[82] Sincerity meant not striving for "effect"; it meant speaking in one's own voice and of one's own vision; it comprised "all those qualities of courage, patience, honesty and simplicity which give momentum to talent, and determine successful Literature." Those who paraded in borrowed ideas or phrases, like those who sanded their sugar, might succeed for a while; they might even live and die respected; yet, Lewes insisted, "it is not a success which a noble soul would envy." True success would come only when one's faculties were employed with sincerity and if one were "appointed" to it. Whatever your vision of the admirable and beautiful, that take as your model, he enjoined.

Whether or not the "public" would appreciate that vision no man could foresee; "enough for you to know that you have done your best, have been true to yourself, and that the utmost power inherent in your work has been displayed."

Lewes insisted that a work must be sincere in style as well as in content. His condemnation of affectation and fine-writing must be taken for what it was: a condemnation of the immoral abuse of style, of the use of appearance to deceive the reader concerning the reality of the vision embodied in the work. Style was not to be denigrated, of course, for more writers had won distinction and immortality through style than through vision, since great dynamic thinkers were rarer than brilliant refiners of the ore. And such a great dynamic thinker as Kant was "not simply unwise, he was extremely culpable in sending forth his thoughts as so much raw material which the public was invited to put into shape as it could." Kant could have taken greater pains to be clear, Lewes felt, although he realized that style was "not an accomplishment but a talent," and that it was not given to everyone to be able to select the "fittest verbal symbols by which they [these ideas] can be made apparent to others." When he tried to give advice on style, therefore, Lewes could do no better than pronounce the "laws" of economy, simplicity, sequences, climax, and variety. Each author, he recognized, had a store of "empirical rules, furnished by his own practice, and confirmed by the practice of others." A true philosophy of criticism, however, he declared, "would reduce these empirical rules to science by arranging them under psychological laws, thus demonstrating the validity of the rules, not in virtue of their having been employed by Cicero or Addison, by Burke or Sydney Smith, but in virtue of the constancies of human nature."

It was a noble goal, but the "Principles" did not achieve it. The laws of style that Lewes recommended were no more than *ad hoc,* empirical, and commonsensical injunctions. The scientific nature of the projected philosophy of criticism was compromised also by appeals to "instinct" and "sincerity"; it was the "selective instinct of the artist which must tell him when his language should be homely, and when it should be more elevated." Variety could be achieved only by obedience to "the great cardinal principle of sincerity"; the writer must be "brave enough to express himself in his own way, following the moods of his own mind, rather than endeavouring to catch the accents of another, or to adapt himself to some standards of taste." Thus, the attempt to formulate a systematic literary theory dissolved in the *aqua regia* of empiricism and moral concern. In fact, the "Principles" was written out of a concern regarding the predominance of bad, that is insincere, literature. There were always far fewer voices than there were echoes. If the injunctions in "Principles" reduced two-thirds of mid-Victorian writers to silence, it would have been a result that Lewes would have welcomed with great satisfaction. But one might well wonder why he entitled his article the "Principles of Success in Literature"; why not the "Principles of Excellence" or even simply the "Principles of Literature"?

It may be that middle-class Victorians required a theodicy of success: that is to say, they needed to be assured that character, perseverance, sincerity, authentic vision, and similar noble qualities were the prerequisite of success, in order to draw the inference that their success was indeed the result of such admirable qualities. As Max Weber shrewdly noted in his "Social Psychology of the World Religions": "the fortunate is seldom satisfied with the fact of being fortunate. Beyond this, he needs to know that he has a *right* to his good fortune. He wants to be convinced that he 'deserved' it, and above all, that he deserves it in comparison with others. He wishes to be allowed the belief that the less fortunate also merely experiences his due."[83] Social Darwinism, Samuel Smiles's gospel of self-help, and Lewes' "Principles" may be read as the various forms in which the theodicy of success appeared. The need of the successful middle-class was not only for the self-serving and self-congratulatory aspects of these doctrines, but also for simple assurance, for certainty in the face of the contempt of their social superiors and in the face of the uncertainty of a good fortune unconsecrated by tradition—a good fortune, if Thackeray's novels are any indication, alarmingly susceptible to sudden ruin. These may have been some of the subconscious reasons why the grandson of a comedian and great-grandson of a hosier chose to call his essay in aesthetics the "Principles of Success in Literature."

The intellectual reason for the emphasis on "success" was, of course, its empirical nature. In 1846 Lewes had written about Lope de Vega that his "mere popularity is an evidence of prodigious talent." To belittle his works, as many critics had done, was "to misconceive the nation that applauded them." The "unexampled success" of Lope and the endurance of his plays through time and change would convince any unbiased person that he was a writer of some power. "He would conclude this," Lewes declared, "without looking at the works. The fact itself would be sufficient."[84] How far was success a "test of merit"? he asked rhetorically, and answered: "Rigorously considered, it is an absolute test. . . . We may lay it down as a rule that no work ever succeeded . . . even for a day, but it deserved that success; no work ever failed but under conditions which made failure inevitable."

To discover the conditions for success was therefore to find the conditions for good literature.

The most obvious difficulty with the notion of success as a test for literary merit was the necessity to distinguish between dishonorable success and the kind of success that befitted a "noble soul." The success acquired by dishonesty, deception, and insincerity had to be set apart from the success of true vision and sincere style; Lewes made the distinction by flat assertion rather than by argument. Similarly, there was the problem of evaluating the success of the crude, sensationalistic novels of the day, or the riotous extravaganzas that passed for drama. Such works appealed to the public's craving for excitment and amusement. Although Lewes had on several occasions deplored all pandering to public vulgarity, he was inclined in "Principles" to treat these questionable successes leniently; only posterity, he said, could decide whether they were enduring successes or not, and it was not for writers to produce for posterity. "*Margaritas ante porcos!* is the soothing maxim of a disappointed self-love," he said. "But we, who look on, may sometimes doubt whether they *were* pearls thus ineffectually thrown; and always doubt the judiciousness of strewing pearls before swine." These hard words betrayed the Victorian belief that talent, like water, would find its own level; it was the literary equivalent of social Darwinism, a doctrine of the survival of the fittest in art.

The static nature of success posed another difficulty in using it as a yardstick for literary merit. As Lewes was well aware, audiences lagged behind great art: "A masterpiece excites no sudden enthusiasm; it must be studied much and long, before it is fully comprehended; we must grow up to it, for it will not descend to us."[85] One might well ask whether Lewes would have taken the trouble with the Elgin Marbles or *Faust*—both of which, he confessed, made no great impression on him at first—if he had not known beforehand of the consensus that they were masterpieces. Closely related to this question was the serious problem of how a new masterpiece might be received by an aesthetics based on past successes. It was not a problem which received attention from Lewes in "Principles," but elsewhere he provided some hints as to his position. "The prophet," he wrote in *Problems,* "must find disciples. If he outrun the majority of his contemporaries, he will have but a small circle of influence, for all originality is estrangement."[86] Quite clearly, he believed that novelty and genius had to prove themselves. He himself tried to sponsor new talent such as Robert Buchanan. And he was particularly concerned about the reception accorded George Eliot. Of a laudatory review of *Adam Bede* he wrote, "The nincompoop couldn't see the distinction between Adam and the mass of novels he had been reading. This made me fear that . . . the public would not discriminate a work so truthful and artistic."[87]

Those who did not enjoy special consideration from Lewes would have to take whatever comfort they could from his general remarks. Expanding from George Craik's epigram that there could be no Aristotle without a Homer, he argued in the 1840's that aesthetics had to be created afresh after each masterpiece. In 1853, when Comte's influence was ascendant, Lewes seemed to imply that a new "closed world" (Alexandre Koyré's phrase) of aesthetics would emerge in the positive era, when "the fine arts will find a new scope and new attributes, as soon as their genius shall have adapted itself to the new intellectual systems." But as Lewes was giving more time and thought to the positivist reconstruction of the Victorian cosmos (in the late 1860's), he grew less sure of the science of criticism, reverting to his "evolutionary" stance of the 1840's; the laws of art were not as readily ascertainable as the laws of nature, he said, for "art is in a state of perpetual evolution, new forms arise under new conditions, and new inventions introduce new laws."[88]

This state of flux implied either a kind of natural selection in art in which aesthetics had continually to adapt itself—in which case one might well ask just when the principles governing the "eternally true and necessarily pleasing" would be settled upon—or the dissolution of the science of criticism in an unsystematic empiricism. Here the third and most serious difficulty with success as an aesthetic criterion becomes apparent; there was no countervailing systematic concept in Lewes' essay in aesthetics to be set against the empiricism of success. Vision, the artistic equivalent of the "ideal construction," might have availed, but Lewes did not press it into service. The result in Lewes' own criticism was a forced revaluation of authors like Fielding, Dumas, Balzac, and Dickens—against all of whom Lewes had reservations on intellectual or moral grounds. Thus, although he considered that *Tom Jones* owed its fame to the fact that it was read chiefly by impressionable and inexperienced youths, he felt compelled to come to terms with it critically because of the "consecration of success" upon it. And he defended Dumas, whose "hysterical romances" he once thought were perversions of truth and history; those who wailed about neglected genius and despised Dumas, Lewes said, did not understand that a man became "distinguished in virtue of some special talent properly directed; and that their [own] obscurity is due either to the absence of a special talent, or to its misdirection."[89]

In the case of Dickens, Lewes' criticism was painfully self-contradictory. "Dickens in Relation to Criticism" was the last essay in criticism that he wrote, and in its perception of Dickens' strengths and weaknesses it reflects Lewes' maturity, but it also conveys the unpleasant impression that Lewes was speaking out of both sides of his mouth. The article was ostensibly a defense of Dickens from those critics who would judge him by false criteria. The great success of Dickens' novels, Lewes said, required to be explained and not merely to be carped at. But the "defence" was as devastating as it might have been if he had intended it to be an attack, which was how John Forster read the essay. In the first place Lewes remarked of Dickens' powers of imagination that "in no other perfectly sane mind . . . have I observed vividness of imagination approaching so closely to hallucination." He denied, of course, any implication that Dickens was insane, but, at the end of the article he narrated two anecdotes which Dickens had told regarding his dreams which, left without comment, strongly suggested something unusual if not abnormal about the novelist's mental faculties. Furthermore, Lewes wrote that the flatness of Dickens' characters reminded him of "frogs whose brains have been taken out for physiological purposes, and whose actions henceforth want the distinctive peculiarity of organic action, that of fluctuating spontaneity." Finally, he appeared to defend the "pervading commonness" of Dickens' works by arguing that only the fastidious paused to remark the lack of "glimpses of a nobler life," yet his essay ended with a highly damning observation that those who, like Lord Jeffrey, have been deeply affected by the presentation of Little Nell — which most "critical readers" pronounced "maudlin and unreal" — were like those who, "unfamiliar with theatrical representations," applauded "an actor whom every play-going apprentice despises as stagey and inartistic."[90]

To be sure, Lewes correctly found the source of Dickens' success in his "overflowing fun," his vivid imagination — the "glorious energy of imagination" which he had in common with all great writers — and the fact that "he spoke in the mother-tongue of the heart." Dickens "painted the life he knew, the life every one knew"; there was nothing ideal or heroic in his novels, "but all the resources of the bourgeois epic were in his grasp." These attributes gave his works the great emotional power which moved people from all classes of society, including the critics who were irritated at their technical defects. But it created a problem for Lewes; he had to explain how, in Dickens' case as in Balzac's, success could accompany such glaring faults. The mere assertion that the "power" of these artists was such that the faults were overshadowed had not much intellectual content to it. Lewes appeared to have had no recourse but to express an empirical and subjective view of criticism.[91] He faulted Dickens for not connecting his observations into a "general expression," for not being interested in the "general relations of things." But he himself had to say that "in matters of Art, there is always a great difficulty, sometimes a sheer impossibility, in passing from the individual to the universal." On the other hand, he continued, it was impossible to resist "feeling": "If an author makes me laugh, he is humorous, if he makes me cry, he is pathetic."[92]

This was nothing less than a retreat into subjectivity and impressionism. Yet the essay on Dickens was highly intelligent and perceptive. Perhaps Lewes' commonsense kept him from pressing into service the superficial and mechanical analysis he had recommended in "Principles." Like his reflections on the science of society, his essays on the nature of literary theory lacked the concentrated, sustained effort necessary to reckon with the divergent tendencies and notions which were common stock in Victorian intellectual life. Though he failed to provide the aesthetics necessary for a scientific criticism, Lewes attended conscientiously to his responsibilities as literary "taster." He also expended much effort, especially in the 1840's and in the early 1850's, in the attempt to introduce the Victorian reading public to literatures other than their own, and he gave to his contemporaries and to posterity *The Life of Goethe*. The mere attempt to write a literary theory, failure though it was, bore witness to a mind restless in its quest for an understanding of the form beneath the shifting appearances of the moral and intellectual universe.

3 / The Construction of a Victorian World-View

We are slowly beginning to recognise that there may be a science of History, a science of Language, a science of Religion, and, in fact, that all knowledge may be systematised on a common Method.

George Henry Lewes

The Victorian interest in science and philosophy was part of its interest in general culture, and for a while books on these subjects fell into the general category of letters. There were, to be sure, works of a specialized and technical nature, which increased in number towards the latter half of the nineteenth century. But Victorian periodicals such as the *Edinburgh* or the *Cornhill* were admirably catholic in their coverage, and writers such as Darwin, Huxley, Spencer, and Lewes himself wrote even their more specialized works with a view to general readership. The meetings, papers, and especially the presidential addresses of the British Association fully reflected the interest and participation of amateurs as well as specialists. Most of Lewes' articles are readily comprehensible to the ordinary reader; some of his books such as the *Physiology of Common Life* and parts of the *Aristotle* and the *Problems* are more demanding. The *Physiology* was aimed at students of the subject, of course, but the descriptions and analyses of physiological theories in *Problems* were part of Lewes' attempt to construct for a wider public a general conception of mental processes.

The major intent of Lewes' work was not obscured by occasionally arcane discussions: he aimed to construct a view of man and of things, a world-view. Like his criticism of society and literature, his writings on science and philosophy were imbued with moral concerns and greatly exercised by the rival claims of empiricism and universality. These rival claims were, naturally, dealt with more explicitly and comprehensively in essays on science and philosophy than in articles on literature and society, but the considerations were the same. To deal with Lewes' literary criticism without due assessment of his writings on science and philosophy would produce an incomplete impression of his overall philosophical intentions and outlook. His non-literary writings are as extensive as his literary criticism, and together they provide a clear understanding of his motives and achievement: he shared the general Victorian sense of need for a reconstructed world-view and the vague expectation that the methods of science would prove equal to that task. He tried to contribute to it by singling out key problems which he attempted to resolve by "reasoned realism." His early writings were more scientistic, almost millenarian in their sanguine expectation that science would provide every needed answer. His later writings appear more mature in their attempts to articulate a "meaningful cosmos" amid some uncertainty.

Science as Paradigm

To a large extent in Victorian intellectual life, science set the standard against which all other categories of truth and knowledge had to be judged; its method was pronounced to be the panacea for all intellectual problems. Ever since the time of Bacon, natural philosophy had shown the physical universe to be the work of a divine Designer, and the book of nature a supplement to revealed scripture and thus a respectable object of inquiry. The development of natural theology, on the other hand, contributed to the symbiosis of science and religion. By the middle of the nineteenth century, however, science appeared to have subverted the received wisdom of the age. Higher criticism and the theory of natural selection might well have appeared as indications of the *trahison des clercs,* had not many of the scientists and intellectuals made prodigious efforts at accommodation and conciliation. Almost every periodical devoted to general culture published articles which attempted to explain, and often to explain away, the results of science.[1] Thus a man of letters able to turn out articles related to scientific subjects might enlarge his scope (and his income). Lewes wrote a great many scientific notes and short articles for the *Leader* in the early part of the decade, mainly attacking various "enthusiasms"—spiritualist seances, clairvoyance, and such vulgar, untenable notions as spontaneous combustion.[2] Some of his articles had the unpleasant, unduly self-important tone of an amateur masquerading as an expert—his attack on Dickens' view of spontaneous combustion, for example, and his scepticism about phrenology, which annoyed Charles Bray. But on the whole they, like his literary criticism, were lively, informative pieces.

Lewes' biography of Goethe discussed his forays into optics and botany fully and sympathetically. In the 1850's Lewes himself conducted a series of "sea-side studies" which were published in *Blackwood's* and, subsequently, as a book. His *Physiology of Common Life* also first appeared as articles in *Blackwood's.* In 1868, on a visit to Heidelberg and Bonn, he noted with gratification that both books were "universally known to men of science." In the 1860's, Lewes published *Studies in Animal Life* and *Aristotle,* as well as numerous minor pieces in the *Cornhill* on popular, semi-scientific subjects such as "Phosphorous and Civilization," "On the Future Extinction of Blue Eyes," and "Training in Relation to Health." There is no doubt that many of his scientific articles were sparked by journalistic opportunism. He once confided to his journal that one of his "regrets at the idea of finishing the Physiology [of Common Life, published in 1858-1860] was lest I should not find a paying scientific subject to take its place."[3] Science was also a serious matter, and many of Lewes' works were concerned with his own discoveries and with the appropriation of the scientific method for the construction of a cosmology. Even his potboiling, however, often had a higher purpose. When he ridiculed spiritualism, spirit-rapping, table-turning, and other Victorian enthusiasms, it was to assert the importance of discrimination in evaluating "evidence." The spontaneous combustion attributed to excessive alcoholism, Lewes declared, was simply impossible, regardless of the number of witnesses and authorities; and, as for spiritualism, "the evidence of the senses is not to be trusted, when they report anything so absurd as that. I would not believe such a thing if I were to see it — the absurdity is too glaring."[4]

That overstatement of common sense — what Comte called *bon sens vulgaire* — as opposed to mere empiricism was an outburst of the masculine Victorian intellect, not a philosophy of science. As a man of letters, Lewes felt it his duty to act as guardian of the intellectual and cultural life of his readership. In a less outraged moment, Lewes urged that it was necessary to maintain a healthy scepticism, and personally to verify particular findings or, at least, to be discriminating in one's choice of authority. The need for such caution was ever present in biology; of all sciences it was the most complex and, for that reason, "preeminent as a means of culture." He was willing to expand the role to include all scientific activity as this "means of culture," by which he meant something like the training of the mind. William Hamilton in his *Lectures on Metaphysics* had argued that philosophy—that is to say, speculative reasoning—was the preeminent means as it involved the search of knowledge for its own sake. Lewes replied that, just as a boy would quickly recognize the futility of attempting to catch a swallow, so any activity with hopelessly unachievable goals (such as those of philosophy) should be abandoned. In the recognition of limitations and in the exercise of searching after the possible by vigorous and disciplined mental activity, science was without peer as an "element of culture."[5]

Lewes was interested in science not merely as a mental tonic; in his serious works he attempted to expand the borders of physiological knowledge, to inspire others to the study of nature, and to apply the scientific method rigorously to critical aspects of human life and mind. His *Aristotle* was an exposition of the scientific works of the Greek philosopher and contained many striking statements on the nature of the scientific method. The *Sea-side Studies* claimed to advance "new facts and new physiological interpretations," and was presented in a popular style. Lewes recognized that the motives for undertaking the study of natural history were a "simple delight in natural objects" and an interest in making philosophic inquiry into the complex facts of life; as a good journalist, he knew how to exploit such motives. Despite the "soft sell" of these studies, however, he expected that the "physiological novelties" he presented would be appreciated by "every competent person" as the "result of hard work and continuous application." His *Studies in Animal Life,* too, was a popularization with an underlying serious intent. In a somewhat lyric tone, Lewes invited his readers to a contemplation of the animal world:

Come with me, and lovingly study Nature, as she breathes, palpitates, and works under myriad forms of Life—forms unseen, unsuspected, or unheeded by the mass of ordinary men. . . . Avert your eyes a while from our human world, with its ceaseless anxieties, its noble sorrow, poignant, yet sublime, of conscious imperfection aspiring to higher states, and contemplate the calmer activities of that other world with which we are so mysteriously related.

Such were the blandishments he used to coax his readers to consider frogs, parasites, worms, and *infusoria* worthy of the attention of a serious person. "The life that stirs within us is also the life within them," he argued, to further his point that the study of such less noble creatures would significantly supplement the study of man.[6]

The Physiology of Common Life (1858-1860), though published in part as articles in *Blackwood's,* was far less attractively written than the other two series of studies. In it Lewes attempted to sum up current physiological doctrines regarding blood, nerves, respiration, nutrition, and other parts or functions of the body. There is an argumentative tone from time to time which enlivened what was quite dry-as-dust. The book made no real contributions to physiology, but it was presumably serviceable as a digest of current physiological knowledge. George Eliot reported that it was "much in request among medical students." A Russian translation was said to have inspired Pavlov to study physiology. The only contribution, however, that Lewes is now considered to have made to physiology was a theory of "muscular sense"—that certain "sensations" originated in the muscles, as opposed to the brain or the skin. This was the substance of one of three short papers read on his behalf at the meeting of the British Association at Aberdeen (1859). The papers created a "row"—to Lewes' delight; he was also pleased to hear that Huxley had defended them.[7] Lewes' delight at the reception given to his papers shows that, though his forte was exposition and popularization and his sallies into "original" ground served mainly to spice up an otherwise boring genre, he wanted to be able to identify himself with the Victorian culture hero, the dis-coverer, by making findings of his own. His exposition of Comte's philosophy of the sciences purported to contain an updated knowledge of science, even taking issue with the master himself on a few points; in his articles on Darwin's *Origin,* where the subject itself was of vital interest to his readers, he could not refrain from adding his own embel-lishments.[8]

That Darwinism was responsible for greatly accelerating the erosion of religious faith was a view widely held among the Victorians, and by some historians, although it is not clear how one might verify such an assessment. Darwinism was naturalistic and non-teleological, and it therefore forced many educated Victorians to think of the universe in a frighteningly new way. For they had an obsession about the rationality of the universe, which they associated with the notion that the universe was under the watchful guidance of a higher power: Providence. Darwin's hypothesis not only provided a naturalistic explanation for one of the major puzzles of early nineteenth-century biology, the problem of species; it also struck at the foundations of the notion of a providential universe. Natural selection would explain the apparent harmony of the world not as the result of design or intelligent intervention, but as the result of an optical illusion, as it were, which consisted of looking at a slice of the earth's history rather than at its dynamic development.

Godwin had rejoiced to find that there were never more people than there was enough food for, and concluded that this was a "principle in human society." But Malthus pointed out that that happy state was the result of the deaths of those for whom there was not enough food.[9] Similarly, Darwin stood natural theology on its head and argued that the apparent design and harmony were only a two-dimensional view of the internecine struggle waged at prodigious cost by the earth's inhabitants in the course of history. The reality made a grim picture; and, although Darwin tried to convince himself in the *Origin* of the eudaemonistic aspect of natural selection — that, as it "works solely by and for the good of each being, all corporal and mental endowments will tend to progress towards perfection" — his *Autobiography* reveals a horror at the wastefulness of the process and its incompatibility with the idea of an omnipotent and benevolent Providence.[10]

Most of Darwin's critics refused to see the point of his theory of Natural Selection. If they accepted his explanation of variation and selection, they nonetheless focused their attention on the effective variations, the survivors; the notion that new species developed through trial and error, as it were, was rejected out of hand. Thus the Duke of Argyll, in his popularly received *Reign of Law,* argued that Darwin's theory was compatible with Design; for though the many factors involved in natural selection each operated in accordance with naturalistic laws, their very multiplicity allowed for, indeed required, the operation of a higher mind which decided upon the combination of these factors. Above all, the Duke stressed the adaptive aspect of variation and avoided coming to terms with the weeding-out process involved in natural selection. Lewes, who belonged to a small group of tough-minded, non-religious intellectuals and had no stake in the notion of a providentially designed universe, looked at the matter from an entirely different angle: "Why, with a whole universe at her disposal, should Nature be economical?" he asked.[11] But he was much more interested in the naturalism of Darwin's hypothesis, in the validity of hypotheses in general and Darwin's in particular, and in an embellishment of his own upon the theory of evolution.

As a positive philosopher, Lewes urged upon his readers a naturalistic or positivistic interpretation of the cosmos. He saw in the *Origin* a valuable instance of the transformation of metaphysical explanations into positive ones. Yet, it was with a certain coolness that he welcomed Darwin's contribution. We find Lewes reading the *Origin* in January 1860, with a review for *Blackwood's* in mind. His first analysis of it actually appeared in the *Cornhill,* in an article subsequently republished in *Animal Studies.*[12] In this discussion, Lewes agreed with Darwin on the question of the fixity of species; he argued that the notion of species was only a generalization from individual characteristics and that the unconscious reification of this abstraction in the thinking of naturalists had made it difficult for them to see how species might have originated without supernatural intervention. The development of new species was like that of new languages, Lewes said, citing Friedrich Max Müller's essay on comparative mythology (1856), or like the development of means of transport—from coachroad to tramroad to railroad.[13] In 1861 he decried the rival tendencies, among "conservative minds" to reject the theory as "revolutionary" and among "insurgent minds" to accept it eagerly as "destructive of the old doctrines." He offered a conciliatory viewpoint: that the view of Creation belonged to a different order of conception and required a different order of evidence from that of Darwin's hypothesis. And he gingerly suggested that "if the hypothesis be also true, any seeming contradiction must soon fall away, since no one truth can be at variance with another." It was what Ellegård aptly called the two spheres doctrine regarding science and religion.[14]

Nor was Lewes entirely satisfied with the message of the *Origin*:

when stated in general terms, that hypothesis has a fascinating symmetry and simplicity; but no sooner do we apply it to particular cases, than a thick veil of mystery descends, and our pathway becomes a mere blind groping toward the light. . . . Ten years ago I espoused the [development] hypothesis, and believed that it must be the truth; but ten years of study, instead of deepening, have loosened that conviction.[15]

Ten years before, his knowledge of Spencer's work must have been a major factor in his acceptance of the development hypothesis; for in March of 1852 Spencer's article, entitled "The Development Hypothesis," appeared in the *Leader* — "insignificant in length, but significant in matter," in the words of its author. Huxley had not been convinced by Spencer; Lewes' mind, on the other hand, was predisposed toward a doctrine of development. He had, in 1850, defended Robert Chambers' *Vestiges of the Natural History of Creation* against the attacks of Adam Sedgwick, arguing that the hypothesis was plausible and "convenient" even if it was far from the truth. It could only be appreciated, he declared, by those who, "to unusual knowledge of philosophic zoology, add a power of discerning the value of generalizations even when amid erroneous details."[16]

Furthermore, Lewes in the 1850's and earlier was under the spell of the idea of progress. It was in this form that the concept of evolution first appealed to his mind, so that he had no trouble grasping the drift of Spencer's argument.

Indeed, there is something ironic about his acceptance of Spencer's Lamarckian view of development, which was basically "metaphysical": it merely asserted that animal forms (or social groups) developed from simple to complex, from lower to higher, without explaining how or why. For this reason, Huxley remained unconvinced until Darwin revealed the mechanism for the transmutation of species. When Darwin's theory was published, however, it evoked in Lewes a sense of *déjà vu*. In his most extended discussion of the subject, Lewes spoke of Darwin's hypotheses as "a larger and more philosophic view of the law of Adaptation which Lamarck had imperfectly conceived" or even a logical extension of the earlier doctrine of Epigenesis. Lewes' view of biological evolution was not quite Lamarckian; but the principle of natural selection was lost in the larger vision of evolution, cosmic and social, and he failed to appreciate Darwin's special contribution to it. Interest did not in fact shift from evolution in general to natural selection in particular until the early 1870's, and even then, the complex and technical nature of the discussion put it beyond the grasp of most people.[17]

A great deal of public interest centered on the hypothetical nature of the *Origin,* and Darwin was popularly criticized for "neglecting induction in favour of a deductive and hypothetical speculation." In the course of those mid-Victorian years, the majority view regarding the nature of hypothesis in science was shifting away from the vulgar notion that science was merely a description of facts; both William Whewell and John Stuart Mill, the idealist and the empiricist poles of thought on these matters, were agreed that Newton's much-quoted dictum, *hypotheses non fingo,* was not to be taken at face value.[18] Lewes played a part in the change by urging a more "philosophic" view of science upon his readers. Reviewing Liebig's *Familiar Letters on Chemistry* in 1851, he lamented the absence of "general *ideas*" and "philosophic accuracy" in the midst of a wealth of facts; in his article on "Goethe as a Man of Science," he praised the architects of science as opposed to the brick-layers, and declared that the *a priori* method, scorned in England by "pretended Baconians," was in fact "one of the most effective [weapons] in the armoury of science," pro-vided, of course, strict rules of verification were observed. In his *Sea-side Studies* he derided the lists of details which crowded Victorian books and journals as "no better than the observations of Chaldean shepherds, which produced no Astronomy in centuries of watching"; and in his *Problems of Life and Mind,* Lewes declared that science was "essentially an ideal construction very far removed from a real tran-script of facts."[19]

To Darwin's hypothesis, however, Lewes recommended a modification: he argued that natural selection depended too much on kinship; he wanted room made in any develop-ment hypothesis for consideration of "conditions" or "medium." Thus the similarity discernible among certain chemicals (like that among some nations) cannot be explained on grounds of kinship and must be attributed to similarity of conditions. The same kind of explanation might be serviceable for phenomena in the animal and vegetable kingdoms. And, if similarity could be attributed to the influence of the medium, then it could further be argued that evolution was multiple — had multiple origins, and "multiplicity of divergent lines."[20] The "medium" must be considered as well as the organism, but it should be defined as broadly as possible in order to withstand the arguments of those who, like Louis Agassiz, believed that the influence of merely physical conditions upon the existence of organisms was minimal, since "the most diversified types of animals and plants are everywhere found under identical circumstances." Against this, Lewes asserted that if one considered *everything* that would affect the organism —and here he called upon Claude Bernard's notions of the *milieu extérieur* and the *milieu intérieur*—one would find that the circumstances were not identical.[21] As Lewes understood it, Darwin's theory implied the evolution of "organic substance" in only one spot; and while that made a "formula of speculative beauty," it involved an "immense improbability."[22] The doctrine of multiple origins* might appear similar to that of successive creations, but there was a critical difference: the former was positivist and naturalistic, the latter presupposed a force external to matter.

Darwin's work also raised questions that troubled the Victorians deeply—whether human beings were part of the animal chain of being, and what the implications of that were for any notion of man's soul, mental faculties, and morality. Although the *Origin of Species* made hardly any references to human beings, it was this aspect which claimed a large part of public interest.[23] Darwin himself did not elaborate upon the implications of his theories of descent and natural selection until 1871 when *The Descent of Man* appeared, somewhat as an anti-climax. But it was clear where the naturalism of the *Origin* would lead: to a doctrine of man as a member of the animal kingdom and of his faculties as similar to, even if improved versions of, ordinary animal faculties. Despite Darwin's caution, this provoked a strong, emotionally negative reaction among Victorian intellectuals.

*Darwin thought highly of Lewes' articles in the *Fortnightly* but was not convinced by his arguments for multiple origins (Charles Darwin to GHL, August 7 and November 18, 1868; I am indebted to Professor Gordon S. Haight for letting me have copies of the Darwin-Lewes correspondence about these articles).

Even those who, like Huxley and Lewes, scoffed at the more tender sensibilities of their contemporaries came up with special distinguishing features for mankind. For Huxley, who made his tough-minded views known in *Evidence on Man's Place in Nature* (1863), it was language; for Lewes it was language and the social medium of which language was both the product and the instrument. Man, Lewes argued, was not only an "Animal Organism," he was also a "unit in a Social Organism," as a result of which he developed faculties that remained rudimentary in animals. For Darwin, the difference was one of degree, and he sometimes doubted if certain of man's mental capabilities, such as the sense of beauty, were better developed than the corresponding capabilities in animals.

Lewes equivocated. It would be as unfair to dwell upon the inconsistencies or equivocations in Lewes' writing as it would be false to fabricate out of all his different ideas a coherent system. Thus, in one of his more comprehensive statements on the problem of distinguishing human from animal intellect, he argued that the notion of a "rational soul" in man was merely a "phrase which did duty for an explanation." But, he continued, it was better than the "crude materialist hypothesis" which did not take into account an *external* factor.* For it was "almost universally admitted that animals and men having similar structures must have similar functions; and further, that the mental manifestations being determined by organic structures, the mental functions of animals and men must be essentially

---

*Lewes was referring to the localizing of the mind in the brain and the attempts to show how the difference in the brain capacities of animals and human beings illustrated (or failed to illustrate) the gap between man and animal (*Problems,* I, 160). Perhaps he also had in mind the famous *hippocampus* debate between Richard Owen and Thomas Huxley and the assertions of the phrenologists.

similar." Yet there existed a gap between animal and human intelligence which could be bridged only by "an addition from without." That bridge, Lewes said, was "the Language of symbols, at once the cause and effect of Civilisation," meaning the social medium. Reaching for a mathematical metaphor, he declared this "addition from without" to be like a second center, creating an ellipse instead of a circle, a difference in kind rather than of degree. Lewes flatly asserted that the social medium—that "collective accumulations of centuries, condensed in knowledge, beliefs, prejudices, institutions, and tendencies"—formed "another kind of Psychoplasm to which the animal is a stranger." It served to explain man's mental and moral distinctiveness.[24]

Religious intellectuals like R. H. Hutton did not think it possible that an altruistic system of morality could have arisen through what appeared to be a basically selfish evolutionary process. But the Darwinian reply was quite simple—that values were selected on the basis of utility for the species as a whole, not for the individual. Thus honesty and loyalty would be found useful in practically any society.[25] To Lewes, who had a clear idea of society as a whole, it was obvious that "impersonal and social" values evolved out of social needs, and that any difficulty in conceiving of such an evolution arose only if society were considered merely an agglomeration of atomistic individuals. As far as Lewis was concerned, that was a false problem; for though society was constituted from individuals, it had a life of its own, and the "collective Experience of the race" molded the experience of the individual; "it makes a man accept what he cannot understand, and obey what he cannot believe," and without it there simply could not be any "moral relations."[26]

The intellect likewise drew "both its inspiration and its instrument from the social needs." Without society, man would be without the *"accumulation of experiences"* which makes possible speculation, conceptualization and other mental activities; man would also be without language, "wholly a social product for a social need" and the instrument for the "world of Thought and Spiritual Insight, of Knowledge and Duty, loftily elevated above that of Sense and Appetite." It was the social medium and its functions, morality and a particular form of mental activity, which distinguished men from animals. There was the logic of signs in addition to the logic of feeling and the logic of images — a three-fold division of mental activity which Lewes borrowed from Comte; animals had no capacity for the logic of signs. This logic was to that of feeling as algebra was to arithmetic, Lewes said, employing a favorite analogy; it was more general and symbolic in nature, substituting "general relations for particular relations."[27] And language made this possible. The role of language in the social medium was like that of the nervous system in the body: as the neural process active today prepares for other processes tomorrow, so the name given to an object or event not only serves to record the fact but also to connect it with other facts, and out of this very connection new light radiates.[28] This felicitous comparison illustrates the nimbleness of Lewes' mind and the arresting way in which he sometimes found analogies in unexpected areas. In the context of his writings on psychology, however, the comparison was particularly apt; for Lewes conceived of scientific enquiry into human intelligence as a two-fold task, involving the study of its physiology as well as the study of its sociology. The implication of Darwin's theories of descent and natural selection had only made more acute the necessity for such an enquiry. Lewes' interest in psychology, which he often treated as though it were epistemology, dated back to the 1840's. But in the

Problems it became clear that epistemology was subordinated to the larger study of those mental faculties and operations which distinguished man from his fellow creatures. His writings on psychology were, of course, inconclusive; he believed it was not yet "constituted" as a science, had not received its place in the "hierarchy of Philosophy" with its object circumscribed, its method settled, and its "fundamental principles" established.

For one thing, there was great confusion over the various concepts of consciousness, feeling, and thought. Lewes wondered if all these could not be better comprehended as different aspects of a single phenomenon—sentience, just as in "vegetable physiology" sepals, petals, pistils, and stamens could all be considered as different aspects of the leaf. This appropriation of Goethe's dictum regarding plants, that all was leaf, had the virtue of enabling Lewes to avoid parceling out different mental activities to different parts of the nervous system; that, he believed, was unsound physiology. "Anatomical and physiological evidence converge to show that cerebrum, medulla, and spinal cord are purely topographical distinctions in the one continuous central axis." This axis he chose to designate as the sensorium, "a plexus of sensibilities"—in other words, "the sum of the conditions requisite for the production of Sentience."[29] As Lewes saw it, this holistic view of the nervous system and of mental activity would circumvent the problems raised by theories of voluntary as opposed to involuntary (or reflex) action, of conscious as opposed to unconscious activity. "I am a conscious organism," he said, "even if it be true that I sometimes act unconsciously. I am not a machine, even if it be true that I sometimes act mechanically." The long and disjointed discussions in *Problems* obscure the point of the work, which appears to be that the explanations of mental phenomena then current—for instance, the reflex theory and the identification of the brain as the organ of the mind—were "crudely materialistic."[30]

That is a startling point of view to discover in a positivist whose life's work was to urge a naturalistic view of the universe upon his contemporaries; it is, however, only the impression given by imprecise language on the part of Lewes, who ought to have distinguished between "materialistic" and "mechanistic." His anti-materialism constituted, in fact, a rejection of mechanistic and simplistic explanations for complex and organic phenomena; it was, to use Owsei Temkin's suggestive distinction, a "vitalistic materialism" like that of the French physiologists and unlike the "mechanistic materialism" of the German physiologists. Lewes insisted that it was not possible to reduce all psychological phenomena to physiological, let alone mechanical, terms. While he objected to the hypostatization of the abstraction, vitalism, he was sympathetic to the general thrust of vitalism, which held that "in the living organism the substances are placed under conditions different from those in which we observe these substances when their chemical affinities are displayed in anorganisms."[31]

Vitality as a function of the entire organism and sentience as that of its entire nervous system—both these holistic notions symbolize Lewes' contention that the complexity of the problems of life and mind would not yield to shortsighted, narrowly circumscribed attacks. Further, arming his position with paradox as well as with logic, Lewes argued that it was the mechanists who, by dealing only with the physiological aspect of mental activity, invited the dualistic notion of a soul inhabiting the body. For, patently, physiology could not explain the subjective aspect of mental activity, and the willful reduction of psychology to physiology had no logical recourse but to posit a second factor. Lewes' solution was to treat both the subjective and the objective as two aspects of a single phenomenon so that consciousness need not be considered "another agent in the series," but only a new aspect. To regard, as Mill did, the neural process as the cause and the subjective process as the result was not only bad physiology, it offended sentiment. In a passage illustrative of Victorian sensibilities, Lewes declared:

What reason regarded as a defective conception [of life and mind, that is, materialism], sentiment dreaded as a moral degradation. Who that had ever looked upon the pulpy mass of brain substance, and the nervous cords connecting it with the organs, could resist the shock of incredulity on hearing that all he knew of passion, intellect, and will was nothing more than molecular change in this pulpy mass? Who that had ever seen a nerve-cell could be patient on being told that Thought was a property of such cells, as Gravitation was a property of Matter?[32]

After the first two volumes of *Problems* had appeared, Lewes attempted to sum up the message of that large work in a two-part article, "Spiritualism and Materialism." He realized that his own views could easily have been perceived by his contemporaries as materialistic or mechanistic; he therefore presented a double defense by carefully distinguishing them from the mechanistic view and by deriding the narrow-mindedness which attached a moral stigma to materialism. He declared that he heartily accepted materialism as "identified with the physiological interpretation" as opposed to the "meta-physiological" interpretation, but insisted that he preferred to speak of his view as a "third school," neither spiritualist nor materialist, "which disengaged what seems valid in each, and by a new interpretation reconciles their differences." His interpretation would be "synthetic" or "organicist," embracing all "cooperant factors." The mind was not to be considered as a function merely of the brain, but of the whole complex organism, "all the parts of which are interdependent, all acting synergetically." Lewes criticized the "agnostics" who evaded the difficulties of framing a theory of life or of mind by "a declaration of its lying beyond science." He himself had, in his article on "Modern Metaphysics and Moral Philosophy in France" (1843), poured scorn on those who enquired into unknowables. But two decades later he had come around to appropriating much hitherto forbidden ground for his philosophy of reasoned realism. True, science — which was to Lewes the same thing as reasoned realism — ought to limit its research to "known functions"; but the arbitrary notion that causes were unknowables was "plausible only through the metaphysical postulate that the cause is something different from its effects." As he saw it, a cause could be known through its effects, and the mysteries of life and mind in particular were accessible through the examination of the vital and mental activities of man.[33]

It was, however, partly this probe into the mysterious which alarmed many educated Victorians. In the *Problems* Lewes tried to assure his readers that science would not rob the universe of its mystery, that scientific conceptualization was an idealizing, noble activity, and that, if indeed science dealt mainly with mundane things, it was vulgar to denigrate it for that reason. In "Spiritualism and Materialism," however, he swung into a posture of attack: "Why," he asked, "should we not rob life of its mystery — if we can?" Those who were "outraged by every attempt to explain moral phenomena by natural laws (which they perversely confound with mechanical laws) [were] urgent in their desire to have all phenomena ultimately referred to moral laws—that is to say, to explain the least complex facts by the most complex."[34] Lewes attacked those who refused to concede the possibility—indeed, the necessity—of explaining moral phenomena by natural laws, those who gave up the natural world as the Second Book of God and retreated into the moral sphere. He intended to bring the fight to them even there. Their escape, he declared in the last article published during his lifetime, "On the Dread and Dislike of Science," was only temporary. Science was beginning its investigations into social and moral relations, and as it had mastered the "principles of physical relations," so would it master the "principles of moral relations." When that happened, Lewes prophesied, "all knowledge will be incorporated in a homogeneous doctrine rivalling that of the old theologies in its comprehensiveness, and surpassing it in the authority of its credentials."[35]

These sharp remarks were a reaction to those who, feeling threatened by the radical redefinitions of great issues necessitated by scientific discoveries, attempted to restrict the scope of rational enquiry. If there were indeed areas in which the scientific method was not competent, and particularly if those areas involved social and moral issues, then the cosmology of reasoned realism would be seriously cramped. Lewes would not abide such a truncation of his philosophy. Interestingly enough, there were those like Frederic Harrison who also desired a more reasonable and acceptable, that is, less "metaphysical," view of men and things, who nevertheless did not think it wise to appeal purely to science. Lewes, however, did not doubt that the physical world and the moral universe could be known comprehensively, meaningfully, and with certainty. He was confident in the capacity of scientific method to come up with objective and absolute truths for the guidance of human thought and activity.

An Empirical Metaphysics

Lewes' interest in philosophy was intense and unflagging throughout his career. Even when he was most violently critical of philosophy, of the traditional systems and modes of philosophical activity, he was insistent that literature, history, science, and indeed all intellectual activity be philosophical: they ought to be part of a larger, more coherent and comprehensive view of men and things. In addition to many articles which dealt directly with philosophy, Lewes also wrote a *Biographical History of Philosophy*, a book expounding Comte's philosophy of the sciences and one on Aristotle, and also *The Problems of Life and Mind,* a five-volume attempt to reconstruct metaphysics. The apparently ambivalent nature of his attitude towards philosophy and the "philosophical" was due to a conflict between his desire meaningfully to comprehend the universe and the predominant intellectual tendencies in England towards an empirical, commonsensical view of things. The English were not fond of the *zu Ende denken* style of continental philosophers. John Theodore Merz, author of a magisterial history of nineteenth-century European thought, observed that "as soon as any argument, however logical it may appear, comes into conflict with common sense, or with strongly held beliefs, it loses its hold of the British mind."[36] As Lewes himself put it in 1846:

Germany and France may style us 'incapable' — 'shopkeepers' — pursuers of the 'practical'; may declare we grovel in the mud because we cannot revel in the sky; it avails nothing: England pursues her steady course, and her sons, as children of the earth, declare they have no wish to leave it for the clouds . . . the *gros bon sens*—the plain practical reasoning of the English Public pronounces Philosophy unworthy of study; and neglects it. Let steady progress in Positive Science be our glory; Metaphysical Speculation we can leave to others.[37]

For many years Lewes maintained this attitude towards any philosophical enquiry which appeared even remotely "metaphysical." In the *Problems of Life and Mind,* however, which was written towards the end of his career, he argued for the acceptance of metaphysics. Hume might have contemplated the impossibility of knowledge, without losing his fabled equanimity, but the Victorians needed the certainty which they so earnestly affirmed—the certainty that "ultimate truths in religion and ethics, in politics, economics, and aesthetics (as well as in the natural sciences)" existed and that the human mind could find them. The avidity with which Lewes expounded Comte and the urgency with which he urged the positive philosophy upon his readers was a measure of his thirst for a satisfying, universal philosophy. Spencer's synthetic philosophy, the most signal Victorian attempt to provide such a system, might be questionable in its materialistic view of the mind, and in its reduction of an explanation of the universe to an assortment of scientific facts and theories. Comte's view of the universe, however, not only promised rigor in its conception and catholicity in its scope, but was also high-minded in its concern for morality and humanity.[38] Although his view of philosophy as the unity of human knowledge was quite classical, the critical aspects of Comte's philosophy—its rejection of theological and metaphysical thinking, its continuity with the "common sense realism of the French Enlightenment"—provided much ground in common with the English tradition. Thus Comte supplied Lewes with the *via media* between the metaphysics so alien to his Victorian sensibilities and the empiricism which he and his generation were slowly beginning to outgrow. Positivism was for him equidistant from mysticism and empiricism.[39]

Nevertheless — and this is a clear indication of the strength of the empiricist tradition — Lewes felt constrained to justify his later philosophical activity. In an issue of the *Fortnightly Review*, which he was editing in 1865, he remarked with a note of nostalgia that the attacks on the philosophy of William Hamilton — most notably that by Mill — would either destroy it or stimulate such an earnest response from its disciples "as to make metaphysical speculation once more a great arena for intellectual athletes, as of old it was." A few months later, in one of his "causeries" in that review, he declared, "I have protested against the pretensions of Metaphysics in terms too explicit to be misunderstood, when I now express satisfaction at the reawakening of an interest in Philosophy." And finally, when he published the first volume of *Problems of Life and Mind* (1874), he conceded that certain problems which he had long declared to be insoluble were insoluble not in themselves but by the method traditionally employed in solving them. With the adoption of a new method, the Method of Science, these problems would be solved. "I propose to show," he declared, "that metaphysical problems have, rationally, no other difficulties than those which beset all problems; and, when scientifically treated, they are capable of solutions not less satisfactory and certain than those of physics." Such a change of mind was not, he asserted, a retreat, but a "change of front."[40]

This change of front has been attributed to the advance of positivism and to the example of Comte's *Système* and similar works of broad philosophical scope.[41] It is also possible, as the philosophical climate changed in the decades between 1850 and 1870, when idealism began to make its presence felt, that Lewes found pressure or inspiration to turn to metaphysics. In any case, he was quite right in denying that his new interests constituted any kind of retreat. In fact, a great deal of continuity exists between his earlier and later works. They all reveal the same blend of scientism and search for a coherent comprehension of the universe (which might be termed metaphysics). In the earlier works, the empiricism was more uncompromising; whole areas were written off as unknowable because they seemed inaccessible to the scientific method. In the later works, this scientism is muted; there was a realization of the incomplete nature of his earlier *Weltanschauung*. What Lewes and the other Victorian intellectuals did not see clearly enough was that scientism was a form of the search for certainty. That certainty, however, had to extend beyond the brute and trivial facts of everyday life in order to provide a satisfactory, "meaningful cosmos."

Scientism had dictated the jettisoning of extra-sensible data and concepts; these Lewes set about to rescue and to establish on a scientific, that is to say empirical, footing in his *Problems*. It is useful to consider here the illuminating distinction that Professor Donald Fleming has made between the "contracted life-style in science" of the Mechanistic Quadrumvirate and the "expansive life-style" of the "medical materialists." Both groups of German scientists deplored the mystification of the life sciences by vitalists; but, whereas the former demanded only enough room to do their research and sidestepped any "cosmic pretensions," the latter claimed that "world riddles . . . could be solved by the same means as the riddles daily unlocked by science."[42] The early and later phases of Lewes' work bear some similarity to these two life-styles, but also show some differences. In the early period, he not only sidestepped cosmic pretensions, he declared them unworthy of speculation — a declaration itself of some cosmic pretension. In his later works, his faith in the omni-competence of the scientific method was as robust as that of the medical materialists, but he resisted the reduction to mechanism or materialism, inheriting from Comte the notion that each of the sciences established in the positivist hierarchy had its own particular version of the scientific method. Nevertheless, the distinction is helpful; the shift from the "contracted" view of the scope of the scientific method to the "expansive" view was the substance of Lewes' change of front.

The most extended of Lewes' attacks on philosophy and metaphysics is his eminently readable *Biographical History of Philosophy,* first published in 1845-1846 by Charles Knight, one of the foremost purveyors of cheap knowledge in early Victorian England, and republished in several, much-expanded editions. The first edition is in Lewes' best "slashing" style. It is clear, compact, and uncompromising, and it begins with the claim of writing as a "sceptic after having been many years a believer." Lewes' belief must surely date back to 1836 and the discussions, in Red Lion Square, of Spinoza, whose philosophy had a great impact on him. Lewes wrote four articles on Spinoza and gave him the pride of place in his history of philosophy as the most rigorous and complete metaphysician. In Spinoza's work, Lewes reported with approval, the inquirer was not dazzled with rhetoric nor confused by illustration. He was, instead, treated as a reasoning being; and the argument was presented with all the clarity and compelling rigor of Euclid's theorems. Spinoza was not answerable on his own grounds,

Lewes declared, and yet he had to be answered, for his conclusions were not credible — they were not "expressions of the thousand-fold life whose enigma he has been endeavouring to solve."[43] The gravamen of Lewes' case was that Spinoza assumed it possible to know *noumena* as well as phenomena. Such an assumption implied that there was knowledge which transcended the sphere of sense and necessitated a method of knowing which could obtain such knowledge. Descartes, Lewes asserted, had assumed that metaphysical truths of this sort could be obtained like geometrical truths — from the mind or consciousness. Spinoza, Leibnitz, and even Kant were all accused of availing themselves of this "pernicious" mode of reasoning. "The inquirer may escape Spinozism," Lewes concluded, "by denying the possibility of metaphysical science; thus, and only thus." If not, the philosophy of Spinoza would be found overwhelming by virtue of its completeness and consistency, and of the nobleness of its inventor's life. If one could accept the "ontological method . . . the results of Spinozism are quite as capable of dovetailing with the needs of a noble life as any other system."[44]

Lewes rejected any rationalist philosophy — he called them metaphysical or ontological without any apparent discrimination. To him, no knowledge beyond that acquired directly or indirectly through the senses could be valid. "To believe in the possibility of knowing 'things in themselves,' " necessitated the belief that "every *clear idea* is the *actual* and *total image* of some thing as it exists in external nature." It would mean believing with Descartes that "the mind is a mirror reflecting things as they are," which Lewes was quick to refute: "the mind is not a passive mirror reflecting the nature of things but the partial creator of its own forms . . . the subjective idea is not the correlate of the objective fact." This is hardly a fair representation of rationalist arguments. Nevertheless Lewes' criticism of Descartes and Spinoza shows an important understanding of the shift of philosophical attention which had occurred in the seventeenth century: epistemology had displaced cosmology; "before deciding on the merits of any system which embraced the great questions of Creation, the Deity, Immortality, and c., men saw that it was necessary to decide upon the competence of the human mind to solve such problems."[45]

This orientation towards *das Erkenntnisproblem* is the background of Lewes' deep and abiding concern for philosophic method. He was convinced that nothing could come out of the metaphysical methods which had been invented and championed in the history of philosophy. Kant's attempt to reconcile the empirical and rationalist traditions did not impress him. The critical theory of knowledge was, to Lewes, "nothing less than a scientific basis for scepticism," — not a term of approbation. He did not see anything resembling a Copernican revolution in Kant's conjunction of subject and object in cognition; it was to Lewes only an extension of the Cartesian method. The post-Kantian idealists fared worse; Hegel was accused of "perverse ingenuity," and the entire tribe of German philosophers dismissed as a "race mad with logic, and feeding the Mind with chimaeras!" Such remarks have a philistine snarl to them which Lewes, in his better moments, regretted and against which he sometimes cautioned. "The degrading of philosophy," he once wrote (1838), "appeals to the superficial who thereby think they are rising *above* it." In the preface to the third volume of his history of philosophy, therefore, he acknowledged that such criticisms constituted "sinning against the office of Historian," but pleaded that it was necessary for the unifying purpose of his work: to show by argument "what History shows by Facts — that to construct a science of Metaphysics is to attempt an impossibility."[46]

Instead of the several metaphysical systems, whose achievements were "rapid and illusory" because they were drawn from the "depths of moral consciousness," Lewes urged the method of science which, though slow, was steady and certain. This was the method of Bacon, the "Father of Experimental Philosophy" and patron saint of Victorian scientism. As Descartes founded modern metaphysics, so Bacon founded modern science. And whereas on Cartesian foundations any number of equally questionable systems might be built, on the method of modern science may be erected only one kind of knowledge — "that, namely, of the reduction of many phenomena to one law."[47] The rather uncritical "Baconianism" of these remarks is, however, deceptive; Lewes was well aware of some of the shortcomings of the method, though, typically, the pros and cons did not coalesce in any modified single judgment but remained independent and seemingly contradictory statements. The defect in Bacon's method was a neglect of deduction — a neglect due to a "deficiency in [Bacon's] mathematical knowledge." Lewes acknowledged that Bacon was correct in neglecting deduction as it was then understood, but not in disregarding it altogether.[48] And, after all was said and done, it was an undeniably great achievement, to have pointed the search for knowledge in a new direction, with a new and ominpotent instrument, induction.

The method of Bacon turned English minds away from fruitless scholastic speculation and enabled them to attend to the task of enlarging man's store of knowledge. Speculation about final causes was eschewed, for such things lay beyond the pale of human knowledge. It was in this tradition of recognizing the limitations to human knowledge that Locke, yet another champion of the new method, appeared to Lewes. "It is of great use to the sailor to know the length of his line," Lewes understood Locke to say, "though he cannot with it fathom all the depths of the ocean." Enough that the line was sufficiently long to serve as an instrument of warning against the shoals upon which intellectual enterprise might founder. Locke's position was thus not scepticism, nor merely empiricism, but positivism; not to despair at the inability of man to know certain things, nor to deny the existence of anything not directly experienced, but to acknowledge that all that can be really known must be founded on experience and that such experience "never could be other than relative — it could only be *our* Experience of things."[49]

Lewes' exposition of Hume shows that he was uncomfortable with the latter's heroic scepticism. He agreed wholeheartedly with the attack on traditional philosophy, but felt that to extend it to religion as Hume did was to confuse the issue. For Lewes believed that the positivist onslaught upon metaphysics could in no way threaten religion, by which he meant not the conventional forms, but a humanistic and universalist comprehension of the cosmos. Indeed, he sought, and thought he found, in positivism a surrogate religion, and this is the key to an understanding of his philosophical activity, shifts and all. In an age "clamorous for faith," Lewes said, religion ought once again to "regulate the evolution" of humanity in order to "express the highest thought of the time, as that thought widens with the ever-growing experience." Of course, that highest thought must present a "conception of the world and physical laws, or of man and moral laws" based strictly upon "scientific induction." For this a reconstruction of metaphysics was necessary.[50] His attack on metaphysics was an attempt to destroy the roots of sectarian as well as unscientific vagaries. With the method of Bacon and Comte, Lewes hoped that knowledge would be placed on a sound footing and that the new philosophy would end all "intellectual anarchy."

This expectation, which infused his history of philosophy and which found lengthy and detailed elaboration as empirical metaphysics in his *Problems,* was most clearly and concisely spelled out in an article heralding the positive philosophy of Comte. "The Modern Metaphysics and Moral Philosophy of France" (1843) was wide-ranging, and pregnant with significant views on the nature of knowledge, science, and hypotheses, which anticipated some of Lewes' later works. It attacked the eclecticism of Victor Cousin, the eminent French philosopher and guardian of morals, dismissed the controversy over materialism and spiritualism, and condemned "parrot science," as Lewes termed the fad of dabbling in science then current—all this as well as providing an exposition of Comte's philosophy. With the advent of positivism, Lewes declared, philosophical activity in France received a new morality where hitherto there had been atheism and materialism.[51] In terms almost Saint-Simonian, he celebrated the coming of the new "dogma" which would replace intellectual anarchy with a unified and coherent view of the world. The juxtaposition of metaphysics and morality is significant; the new philosophy was also the new morality, and the new morality was also the new vision of a meaningful cosmos. As he had revealed in his discussion of Spinoza, he expected true philosophy to dovetail with the "needs of a noble life."

The eclecticism of Cousin, which might have been considered an attempt at such an intellectual (and religious) unity, was itself a witness to and a result of the fragmentation of modern philosophy, Lewes asserted. To attempt, as Cousin did, to combine Scotch induction with Hegelian ontology was like attempting to combine Copernican with Ptolemaic astronomy. The lack of a system into which all areas of knowledge might fit could not be remedied by a philosophy which was a patchwork of truths collected from other systems. "We deny that Eclecticism is ever capable of ascertaining the truth unassisted by some criterion of anterior ascertained truth," Lewes declared. On the other hand, positivism was a philosophy which had such a system of truths, a framework into which new truths and data might be fit if these new elements passed the test. It provided the "correct theory," without which "it would not only be impossible for us to combine our isolated observations, and consequently to draw any benefits from them," but we would also not know the value of our observations and "most frequently the important facts would remain unperceived."

It was the genius of Comte, Lewis said, to have invented not only a method, which was indeed derived from Bacon's, but also a system of knowledge. The method was the product of the last of three stages in the development of civilization; the theological having given way to the metaphysical, the metaphysical was in the process of yielding to the positive. Not only was positivism the last "method"; it was also "the only true one . . . the only one capable of furnishing to man the instrument whereby we may 'interrogate nature' with success." Whatever might be said of the positive philosophy itself, Lewes' estimate of its truth was very much like the various expressions of the conviction of sin and salvation of the Evangelical converts, and his uncritical intuitionism outdid the most debased forms of Cartesianism.

It was the combination of empirical probity and philo-

sophic breadth rather than the social atomism, curiously
styled positivism by Noel Annan, which elicited the sympathetic response of the educated Victorians.[52] That
atomism did exist — as witness Herbert Spencer's exposition
of individualism — and had its epistemological counterpart
in Bentham's "method of detail" to which John Stuart Mill
remained loyal. In the intellectual milieu of mid-Victorian
England, Spencer and Mill played undeniably integral
roles. Although positivism rejected, as they did, metaphysical and theological thinking, it was the strength of
positivism to recognize as well the existence of conceptual
and social "wholes" such as "humanity," and to add an
organic aspect to its critical. Like Unitarianism, positivism
was a half-way house to secularism for those who, for intellectual or moral reasons, could no longer believe in God or
immortality but felt compelled to uphold duty. It claimed
also to provide certainty. Whoever has suffered from uncertainty "in questions moral, mental, social, political, and
international," a positivist lecturer stated, "will rejoice to
find a synthesis based on certainty. . . . It meets all real
human wants, individual and collective; while it sanctions
and enforces a moral discipline, the need of which man con-
stantly feels."[53]

Lewes did much to popularize positivism; when Mill's
enthusiasm seemed to flag in 1847, Comte wrote gratefully
to Lewes that his devotion to the cause was the most satisfactory of all the followers in England.[54] In the 1850's Lewes'
exposition of *Comte's Philosophy of the Sciences* was followed by a stint as "resident Comtist" for the *Saturday Review*. That weekly maintained the celebrated insularity of
English philosophic tradition by ignoring all other continental thinkers apart from Comte. Its writers found it difficult,
by and large, to take the religion of humanity seriously, and

yet they showed a distinct deference towards the positive philosophy which indicated a sympathetic response to it. Organized positivism, however, was not a great success in England; it owed its existence over two generations to the dedication of Richard Congreve, Frederic Harrison, and a few others.[55] It was the spirit of positivism which claimed Lewes' allegiance, and that of others like him: they were iconoclastic, yet sought some sort of social and intellectual order; unattached to any form of religion, yet in need of something in which to believe; unconventional, yet earnest and, withal, moralistic. The positivistic cultus might be too bizarre, and its social dogmas too authoritarian, but its intellectual formulas commanded respect and its appeal to more noble sentiments fell upon receptive minds.

In *Problems,* Lewes no longer hurled anathemas at the misbelievers; his reasoning was reminiscent of Mill's in favor of discussion: "All those who put their trust in the Positive Philosophy must regret that it should alienate instead of alluring speculative thinkers, capable of extending its reach." On a new tack, Lewes argued that it was possible and desirable to appropriate the hitherto taboo area of their speculation — ontology — if one did not accept their method of speculation at the same time:

There is Ontology pursued on the Metempirical Method; and this, like all enquiries so pursued, is necessarily fruitless. There is Ontology pursued on the Empirical Method, and this is Abstract Science, which is occupied with the general laws of Being. . . . It is wholly a question of the manner in which the abstractions are formed.

Lewes argued that ontology or metaphysics would be to science what algebra was to arithmetic. "The objects of Arithmetic are quantities; the objects of Algebra are not quantities but the relations of quantities." By this analogy,

Lewes aimed to prove that metaphysics had a basis in science. Though hard-core empiricists might raise their eyebrows, Lewes sincerely intended not to abandon his scientific ways but to apply the method of science to all questions hitherto eschewed as metaphysical in the hope that this would produce a philosophy worthy of England. For he found no satisfaction in the "essays, not systems" of the English philosophical tradition; the time had come for the grand synthesis, and all to be done very scientifically.[56]

It was necessary, at the outset, to distinguish this new metaphysics from the metaphysics which Comte had relegated to the past in his law of three stages and which Lewes termed "metempirics." Lewes argued that research may be conducted in three directions: into the positively known, such as readily appears to the senses; into the speculative but provable, such as may be inferred or deduced; and into the unknowable, which various thinkers have termed "purpose." This last category was to be banned. "Speculation to be valid must be simply the extension of Experience by the analogies of experiences," and it had to be verifiable. Such concepts as matter, force, cause, and even vital principles, were not to be given up despite their past association with metaphysical philosophy (old sense); positivist metaphysics (new sense) could freely acknowledge their existence for they were "symbols of sensible experiences" and "integrant parts of what I call the Logic of Feeling, before they are raised into terms of the Logic of Signs. They are threads woven into the web of Experience."[57]

In *Problems* Lewes embarked upon a brave program: he earnestly tried to meet the two divergent intellectual demands of his age: the one a seasoned empiricism imposing procrustean measures upon all intellectual activity, and the other a swelling need for a kind of "religious rationalism," a meaningful vision of man and things. Empiricism was being modified, to be sure, and had lost the starkness of its classical, seventeenth- and eighteenth-century forms. Even so, there was an increasing number of Victorians who were not prepared "to sacrifice the reality of the experience represented by morality, art, religion to what appeared to be the demands of positive science for a rigidly naturalistic world." Many of them were sorely tempted to abandon all pretense of rationalism and to rely purely on the "witness of the spirit of man itself." Many, like Tennyson, might acknowledge the intellectual ascendancy of the scientific method and still cling to their battered faith, believing what they could not prove.[58] Lewes' program was more ambitious; he expected to lay the groundwork for a philosophy which could come to terms with both demands of mid-Victorian thought.

In order, first of all, to keep his standing as a positivist, he tried to isolate and eliminate the "supra-sensible," or what his friend Herbert Spencer in *First Principles* (1862) called the unknowable. Lewes recognized that it had played a large part in the history of human attempts to understand and explain the universe. Even Kant had succumbed to the "traditional influence of metempirical conceptions" in falling back on the doctrine of innate ideas and in not recognizing the possibility of an empirical metaphysics. The search for the thing-in-itself was, Lewes said, a "metaphysical fetich." It descended from the old concept of essence "which had replaced the earlier conception of a spirit, or demon, living in the object."[59]

Much the same could be said about the concepts of cause and matter. The idea of chance or fate had given way, Lewes declared, to the concept of cause. Comte had rejected the concept altogether, substituting for it the idea of law, but Lewes urged that, in fact, both concepts could be metempirically apprehended, and, conversely, that there was "an empirical conception of Cause which is the precise equivalent of Law." After all, he reasoned, phenomena presented themselves as dependent on other phenomena; from these dependencies and connections may be abstracted the concept of cause. Lewes did not, as Hume did, conceive of the relationship between cause and effect as only an association made in the human mind; he saw it as real. In the second volume of *Problems*, in which he gave a fuller explication of the concept of cause, Lewes argued in effect for the elimination of the concept. The word was useful; it was the "condensed expression of the *factors* of any phenomenon, the Effect being the *fact* itself." As the antecedent must enter into and become *incorporated* in the consequent in order to be considered a cause, the distinction between antecedence and consequence was "purely logical." Hence he concluded that "Causation is Procession," employing with perhaps unconscious irony that curious theological term whose vagueness had made it suitable as an explanation of the standing of the Holy Spirit with respect to the other members of the Trinity. At first flush, this appears a shameless display of the kind of resolution of philosophical issues by verbal distinctions for which he had condemned Hegel and, indeed, the entire tradition of philosophy. There is, however, a certain logic in Lewes' use of the word "procession": it eliminated the dichotomy between cause and effect, and thus the highly complex problem of the relationship between the two; it transformed problematic sequence into something analogous to an identical proposition. This tendency to reduce complex issues or truths to identical propositions (by somewhat questionable reasoning) was a major strategy in his construction and application of a positivist epistemology.[60]

The positivist assessment of chance, however, needed no such reductionism. Lewes merely argued, borrowing from Aristotle, that the idea of chance was a confession of ignorance of cause, that it meant a focusing of attention on the irregularities, instead of the regularities, of phenomena. Such regularities as might be observed gave rise to laws. In 1844, he criticized the great historian of Rome, Barthold Georg Niebuhr, for "unphilosophically" using the concepts of destiny and Finger of God to explain certain extraordinary events. God, Lewes said, ruled everything, not merely the inexplicable or certain remarkable events. His activity must, thus, be taken as a general condition; human enquiry was into the secondary causes. God was behind everything in chemistry and astronomy too, Lewes remarked pointedly, but no one would cite the Finger of God as an explanation in those fields. In 1867, his remarks on the nature of purpose or design in the world bore some evidence of having been influenced by Darwin. The cosmos, Lewes pointed out, was such a great display of waste that it was hard to see any design in it. One might infer the Creator's purpose but could never verify it. In any case, such inferences — as commonly made in natural theology — were based on the assumption that the Creator acted in a human fashion; could one also apply human moral standards to His deeds?[61] The answer to that question reportedly sent many Victorians into unbelief.

Lewes' discussion of matter serves as a further example of his attempt to de-mythologize, as it were, knowledge. "During the long minority of science," he wrote, "under the Regency of Metaphysics, there was no systematic discrimination of its empirical from its metempirical aspects." Even lately, the human mind has shown its proclivity towards dealing with "abstractions in strange disregard of the concretes they express," he complained; it was a "metempirical" reification of universals.[62] To be considered empirically, the concept of matter could not be thus hypostatized; there was no substratum apart from the qualities of various material objects. Matter could be explained only by an enumeration of its properties and an explanation of these in "their extra-sensible relations," that is, such relations as could with validity be inferred and abstracted from the concrete instances. Only thus could any progress be made. There would, for example, have been no development of electricity as a source of power if there had been continued speculation on its "essence" and nature, instead of experiments designed to test and utilize its various properties.

It was, of course, far easier to condemn the metempirical than to show how an empirical metaphysics could be achieved. Arguments such as these are interesting as period pieces rather than convincing as arguments. Lewes himself realized that a science of knowledge, which he called psychology, still awaited a Bichat or a Lavoisier. On the other hand, he made an extended effort to outline the logic of the scientific method in the first volume of *Problems*. His "rules of philosophising" were mainly derived from the third book of Newton's *Principia* and, with lavish humility, he offered them as "no more than certain general results of philosophic reflection on the conduct of Research." The humility was justified as the rules were little more than the codification of common sense: there was the affirmation of empiricism — "no problem to be mooted unless it be presented in terms of Experience, and be capable of empirical investigation" (rule one); there was the enunciation of uniformitarianism — "each cause must always and everywhere have the same effect; and never more than this" (rule six); and there was the principle of economy — "always to prefer the simplest hypotheses compatible with all the observed facts" (rule fifteen).

As empiricism had demarcated the area of the knowable from that of the unknowable, so the principle of uniformity dictated what the nature of the truth must be: "What we mean when we say that a thing is real simply amounts to this: it will always in such or such relations have such or such modes of existence, and in all similar relations similar modes. This conclusion is as absolute as that two multiplied by three will always be six." This was again the definition of truth as an identical proposition. Uniformitarianism, as expounded by Charles Lyell in his *Principles of Geology* (1830-1833), was empirical, naturalistic, and thus eminently scientific; it therefore exercised a great normative influence on the intellectual standards of the mid-Victorians. As such, it prepared their minds for the reception of *The Origin of Species,* and, translated into the notion of the "universality of natural causation," it became a fundamental premise of Victorian social and anthropological analysis.[63] The principle of the uniformity of nature was not, however, without its ambiguities, and Lewes' presentation evoked Alexander Bain's criticism in the very first issue of *Mind.* Bain argued that nature might be slowly changing and that some day, for instance, water might boil at 250°F; this was, in effect, an argument against "substantive uniformitarianism." Lewes' reply, in the next issue of *Mind,* pointed out that he understood uniformitarianism, not in the sense that things or conditions would always be the same, but in the methodological sense — that there would be "identity of effects under identical conditions." It was a caveat which resulted in an order of truth or knowledge which was of a tautological and rather trivial nature.[64]

Lewes seemed to realize this as he expounded the place

and glory of abstraction and conceptualization—mental activities which often involved the "emergence" of truths in a manner transcending such a limited definition—but the uniformity of nature was the necessary underpinning of his empirical metaphysics, and all generalizations, inferences, and "ideal constructions" had to be reducible to such elemental truths to be considered valid. The related question of the nature of discovery was an even thornier problem, and Lewes himself was aware of the difficulties: "How is it possible to extend knowledge by means of a process which is only valid when it is a re-statement of what is already known?" he asked. "Our exposition of Reasoning may seem to lead to Plato's conclusion that all knowledge is nothing but Reminiscence."[65] It is clear that this dilemma stemmed from a confusion of the method of proof with the "method" of discovery. Discoveries are likely to be made through intuition or serendipity even though their proofs must conform to rules of induction.

In general, Lewes was much more concerned with proof than with discovery—his treatment of originality in art was similarly weak—and his own answer to the question he posed was not very clear. It is difficult, upon reading the *Problems,* to resist the impression that Lewes felt the positivist era would see the reinterpretation of human knowledge rather than the extension of it, that the "closed world" of the scholastics and metaphysicians was not to be replaced by an "infinite universe," but to be appropriated and refurnished as the closed world of positivists. There was, then, a sense of finality in the positive philosophy in general, as well as the finality noted in its science of society; to a large extent this must have accounted for the neglect of the analysis of discovery, despite the fact that Lewes, like the rest of his age, was enthralled by the adventures of discoverers whether their exploits occurred in the laboratory or in the heart of Africa. Lewes was only vaguely aware that, as in art a new masterpiece might redefine aesthetic theory, in science a discovery or new hypothesis might reorder one's conception of the physical universe. His theory of knowledge was basically preformationist, into which he had to incorporate an epigenetic element, and he did not know how to explain the situation.[66] New knowledge, like new political forms, was expected to establish itself.*

A more pressing consideration was that the knowledge which might be derived within such empirical and uniformitarian constraints might be considered trivial, whereas the kind of knowledge which was really worth something transcended such constraints. This was, indeed, as Lewes recognized, the idealist critique of empiricism — that "a rational theory of Nature only deserves the name when its laws are *a priori* and cannot be gained through Experience." Lewes himself was convinced that "the truth of Science is the truth of ideal construction" and not merely data based on sensory perception. He applauded Goethe for his "synthetic manner of looking at Nature," and praised Geoffroy-St. Hilaire for placing "synthesis above analysis"; for science did not consist of mere facts, but of "ideas giving to facts their significance."[67]

It was therefore necessary to ascertain the validity of these "syntheses" — inferences, conceptions, universals, abstractions, and hypotheses. All reasoning involved the substitu-

---

*Lewes firmly believed in the doctrine of epigenesis in embryology (*Aristotle,* 354) and suggested the word "emergent" to describe effects whose processes from their causes were not entirely clear (*Problems,* II, 412-414). However, he did not develop the concept of emergence, and his philosophical writings betray the "preformationist assumption about causality" (A. O. Lovejoy, "The Meanings of 'Emergence' and Its Modes," *Proceedings of the Sixth International Congress of Philosophy* [1927], 20-33).

tion of the relations of things for the things themselves and inference was the "ideal presentation of objects not actually present to sense"; hence the absolute necessity for verification. Lewes was aware that, like inferences, certain forms or categories, as Kant put it, entered into every statement which was not merely factual; he agreed with Kant that "there must be *a priori* conditions which render Knowledge possible." But he denied that these were transcendental, which he understood to mean transcending experience. Kant's error lay in a limited view of experience which did not "admit among the elements of individual Experience the modification due to ancestral experiences, and the influences of the Social Medium." The idea of "ancestral experiences" is one of those intriguing arguments which Lewes employed from time to time without further development or clarification. He seemed to imply that what the "race" has learned in the past was inherited biologically and also that it was "inherited" culturally. The child of European parents inherited an organism "more apt to grasp the results of culture," he said, adopting the Lamarckian view that "what is acquired may be inherited." The "accumulated Experience of the race," on the other hand, was "organized in Language, condensed in Instruments and Axioms, and in what may be called the *inherited intuitions.*" The human organism was influenced both by such ancestral experiences and by its experience in the "social medium" of the present — "every man we meet, every book we read, every picture or landscape we see, every word or tone we hear, mingles with our being and modifies it."[68]

By this expansion of the meaning of the concept of experience, Lewes was able to assert what Kant denied, that *a priori* concepts originated in experience — if not of the individual, then of the society. For him as for Spencer, then, truths were *a priori* only for the individual and not for humanity, and were ultimately derived from experience. Hence empiricism was saved. With the same strategy, though in more cursory fashion, Lewes dealt with such apparently non-empirical preconditions or "transcendental" aspects of knowledge as innate ideas, intuitions, instincts, axioms, and self-evident truths. All of them, he argued, were convenient abstractions which when reified appear to transcend experience; when broken down to their components, treated "psychogenetically," as opposed to psychologically, they are found to be of empirical origins.[69] Lewes considered even mathematical truths conditional, that "their universality is restricted to our universe." The truths of geometry, for example, would not hold in a two- or four-dimensional world, he declared; conversely, he considered the "imaginary geometry" of Lobachevski (the Russian mathematician) logical, but arbitrary and *"not* applicable to objects given in our Experience." That system was useful and might indeed be "proved" some day, but only if there were to be "new sensible experiences and new intuitions, which would bring what is now transcendent and metempirical within the empirical range, and allow new conceptions to be raised from new perceptions." Thus Lewes reaffirmed the principles of empiricism and uniformity.

He realized, of course, that in science as well as in everyday life, conceptualization often involved idealization. "From the Pisgah of *what is,"* he said somewhat picturesquely, "the mind sees what *will be,* or *what would* be if all conflicting movements were allowed to neutralise each other." That is to say, from a knowledge of particular instances, the mind framed a law governing their most general characteristics. One knew that individual planets did not move in perfect ellipses and that the tides at various waterfronts might have greatly divergent and apparently anomalous characteristics, but in both cases there were local factors involved which only modified the "ideal construction" of the laws of planetary movements or of tides. It was this particular kind of idealization which transformed mere perceptions into conceptions, mere sensations into philosophy. From an attempted resolution of a critical issue in epistemology, Lewes vaulted over to a declaration on the human condition. It was this which was the hallmark of man, he declared; in the ideal world man planted his hopes and joys, and found his dignity and power. His pains and pleasures were multiplied in the ideal world: "This is man's spiritual being; who would renounce it for the comparative calm of the most fortunate brute?"[70]

In the chapter on ideal construction in science, Lewes incorporated a discussion of moral types. It included an earnest and characteristically Victorian *cri du coeur* adopted from *The Imitation of Christ:* "Oh, would that for one single day we have lived in this world as we ought!" And that cry of moral aspiration was solemnly viewed as a parallel to the relation between physical laws and physical realities: "We all place before ourselves the ideal of a noble life . . . and we do not look on that ideal as a fiction . . . because we fail to realise it. Like the typical laws of physical processes, these conceptions are solid truths although they exist only as ideals." Although Lewes asserted the importance of moral (and aesthetic) sentiments which "give the impulse to theories, and regulate conduct," he conceded that he could say no more of these sentiments or instincts than that they were found as "facts of human nature" and that "their influences were beneficial." If there were anyone whose soul, "like that of an animal, is unvisited by any suggestion of a life larger than its own . . . by what array of argument could we hope to make him feel what his nature does not feel?" He recognized that moral sentiments had no foundation in positive science and could only appeal to the ambiguous and, though he was unaware of it, disintegrating moral consciousness of the Victorians. But morality appeared to him so peremptory that he was able to answer his own disturbing question with relief: "Happily, there is no such man."[71]

Although the Victorian moral consensus concealed from Lewes the metempirical idealism in his views of morality, it was not sufficient to ward off doubts over the propriety of ideal construction in science and philosophy. Rule thirteen of Lewes' "Rules of Philosophising" was, on balance and despite its peculiar vocabulary, the most representative of his statements on the subject: "Philosophy, being the harmony between the concrete and abstract, the synthetic and its explanatory analytic, demands that everywhere the abstract be subordinate to the concrete in respect to validity, though it is superior in point of dignity." The concept of quantity might be "no less removed from any objective sensible" than the idea of a "Hippogriff," but quantity is an "abstraction from Reals" which was "generalised without transposition" and which therefore "accurately represents objective existences," while the Hippogriff was an aesthetic invention inspired by real perceptions but put together without further reference to reality.[72] Similarly, the difference between the ideal constructions of Hegel and Louis de Lagrange, a French mathematician, was that Hegel's "logic was uncontrolled by Verification." Indeed, the main burden of Lewes' *Aristotle* was the absolute necessity for verification. It was verification which safeguarded the empiricism of philosophic activity. Like bank drafts, concepts and abstractions must be reconvertible into the assets they represent: factual data.[73]

There was, however, one category of philosophic and scientific activity which Lewes felt to be not reducible to sense data and experience — the hypothesis. Hypotheses, such as the calculus and evolution, might not be true, he said; they were, however, "ideal constructions of vast power in scientific research": calculus providing solutions to certain hitherto insoluble problems, and evolutionary theory, making it possible to render intelligible the "vast reach of organic phenomena." The nebular hypothesis, evolutionary hypothesis, and indeed geology as a whole were all "dependent on past causations," and thus "cannot receive verification except by reflection from present causation." Nevertheless, "the grandest discoveries, and the grandest applications to practice, have not only outstripped the slow march of Observation, but have revealed by the telescope of Imagination what the microscope of Observation could never have seen, although it may afterwards be employed to verify the vision." On the same page as this enthusiastic appreciation of imagination, however, Lewes cautioned that such imaginative activity must proceed by "abstraction from concrete experiences" in order to be valid. Prevision must be only an extension of vision, and deduction must rest securely on induction. A hypothesis, he had said elsewhere, is a guess, and "one of the last developments of philosophic culture is the power of *abstaining* from forming an opinion where the necessary data are absent."[74]

Such vacillations and inconsistencies underscore the dilemma Lewes faced; he wished to be neither metempirical nor merely empirical. It was a positivist shibboleth to pronounce the unknowable, the absolute, to be outside the pale of knowledge and any enquiry into that aspect of the cosmos invalid. Yet a comprehensive vision of men and things seemed to require some sort of reckoning with such "supra-sensible" objects. At one point, Lewes' positivism expressed itself in curiously stoical fashion: "Resignation without apathy, is the great practical lesson of Life. Acquisecence without indolence is the great speculative lesson." That gloomy reflection might be a logical consequence of the positivist program of knowledge, and it perhaps struck a sympathetic chord in the spirit of self-denial in the temperament of serious, high-minded Victorians. But it was also a denial of the Victorian faith in progress and an attenuation of the hopes which resided in the scientific method. And if positivism or reasoned realism were to replace the old philosophic systems as a vision and explanation of the universe, it could not effectively do so with the stigma of being incomplete. Lewes could argue that there was a "development of knowledge" just as there was a development of the cosmos, that the limits of knowledge were only temporary, continually receding before the advancing tide of science. New techniques were being discovered, such as spectrum analysis, which allowed man to know more than he did before. But this sort of increase, of a quantitative kind, had nothing to do with the storming of the citadel of the unknown. Lewes insisted that knowledge was limited partly to make a virtue of necessity, but the capacity of the resultant philosophy to satisfy the non-rational needs which motivated the search for a *Weltanschauung* was compromised. He had to admit that it was "no matter of exhilaration, but rather of deep regret, that we find ourselves in an universe of mystery"; he therefore had to articulate a more affirmative posture for his philosophy.[75]

Boldly he enunciated the main burden of the *Problems of Life and Mind:* "The Reasoned Realism of this work denies altogether the assumed distinction between noumenon and phenomenon — except as a convenient artifice of classification by which the *unknowable otherness of relations* is distinguished from the *knowable relations.*" It was an interesting twist to the positivist disavowal of noumena, which he proceeded to modify, somewhat obscurely, thus: "We are led through our psychological analysis back to the synthetic starting-point—namely, that the external world exists, and *among* the modes of its existence is the one we perceive." From this Lewes went on to assert that the Absolute could in fact be known—an assertion which he supported by some rather devious arguments. He declared that relativity furnished a criterion which is "coextensive with the domain of intelligence," while the "opposing principle is productive of scepticism" because it has no such criterion and thus "remains fluctuating, because its data are personal, and cannot be communicated." It is clear that Lewes was arguing against an extreme, Berkeleyan subjectivity which denied any knowledge of the external world, let alone of the absolute. He asserted that "in any rational sense of the terms, things *are* known; and if the Absolute is the sum of things then this Absolute is known." Not without qualifications of course, he conceded, but "knowledge so far as it goes, is certain, absolute, not to be rendered illusory by its limitations."[76] But if that knowledge was certain, then there could be certain knowledge of the absolute as well; for what is known is one aspect, admittedly the phenomenal, of the absolute-noumenal. As Lewes quaintly put it, the "absolute and relative being correlative terms, the one cannot be known without the other." Hence positive knowledge of phenomena meant knowledge, albeit limited, of the absolute. Even that qualification might give way if judged by one of the more cryptic passages in *Problems:* "Feeling is an ultimate: it is that in which all knowledge begins and terminates. . . . Does it not follow that Feeling is the much sought

Thing in itself—the ultimate of search? All things can be reduced to it; but it can be referred to nothing more general."[77]

It does not, indeed, follow, even if feeling were "an ultimate"; for Lewes understood feeling as the fundamental mode of knowing, inasmuch as all knowledge came directly or indirectly from experience—through feeling. The absolute was, however, conventionally understood as an object of knowledge, not a method of knowing. It is possible that he had in mind what he had hinted at earlier in the same volume—a theory of the identity of existence and experience: "Existence, therefore, is objective Experience, and Experience is subjective Existence." Like the two poles of a magnet, he explained in a Hegelian vein, subject and object cannot be separated.[78] If this is so, then he might argue that as feeling was the ultimate ground of knowing, it was also the ultimate ground of being. This was thin philosophical ice indeed, for as Bertrand Russell has pointed out, the empirical position assumed that sensations have external causes which, "at least to some extent and in certain respects, resemble the sensations which are their effects." Lewes asserted the identity of sensation (feeling) and object, as he also asserted the unity of cause and effect. Yet, as Russell asked, how could one be certain that the sensations which we experience were in any way due to their "causes" which we do not experience? Empiricism had no answer.[79]

Whatever the philosophical worth of Lewes' attempt to dissolve the various dualisms—cause and effect, matter and feeling, experience and existence—it is more important to assess his effort in terms of his intentions. He wished to establish reasoned realism as a philosophy worthy of faith as well as acceptable intellectually. Like Comte, he aimed at a universally acceptable and satisfying philosophy, a philosophy both empirical and comprehensive. The sharp disapproval of "intellectual anarchy" seems to suggest that what each had in mind was the organicity and wholeness of intellectual life in the Middle Ages—with modern content and method, of course. As Frederic Harrison, one of the leaders of organized Positivism and a friend of Lewes, remarked, at bottom "mankind really longs for something like a rule of life, something that should embody all the phases of our multiform knowledge, and yet slake our thirst for organic order." Humanity had passed through both the theological and metaphysical ages and was now on the threshold of the positive. The proto-positivists, the men of science, had been shy of applying their method to questions regarding the ultimate, pleading that the solutions were beyond human knowledge. These were men with a "contracted lifestyle in science." Then came Comte, whose philosophy was not only based upon the scientific method but was also the means whereby all further scientific activity—indeed, all human activity—might be comprehended and given its proper place and value. It was therefore time, Lewes said, to abandon "such lavish humility" as the proto-positivists had displayed, for that was "far from admirable."[80] As an indication that his work was free from such false emotion, he entitled the first two volumes of *Problems, The Foundations of a Creed.*

That the Victorian "cosmos" needed to be meaningfully comprehended was something of which the Victorians themselves were acutely aware. Coleridge, Carlyle, Mill, Maurice, Newman, Tennyson, and a host of others each contributed to the voluminous literature which testified to the quest for a philosophy and faith which would enable them to come to terms both with their knowledge of the outside world and with what can best be called their moral consciousness. Lewes had no religion to lose that we know of; yet even he, by protesting so much to have found the answer to the intellectual anarchy of his times, bore testimony to the Victorian crisis of belief. Apparently it was not just conventional religion that was affected by the new knowledge, whether of textual criticism, or geology, or biology. It was the whole body of received wisdom regarding the physical and moral universe which decomposed under the impact of the new knowledge. Victorian men of letters naturally tried to help their contemporaries come to terms with these changes. Lewes' contribution was the advocacy of a combination of the scientific method and a secularized religious concern — a difficult blend, but one preferred by a significant section of the Victorian intellectual community.

Epilogue

Lewes was neither the greatest of Victorians nor the most Victorian of them all. Not so bookish as Leslie Stephen, nor so solid as Richard Hutton, nor so representative in the balance of his interests as Walter Bagehot, Lewes represented perhaps the more effervescent, more eccentric, and yet also the more truly philosophical aspects of the mid-Victorian mind. He was concerned in a general way with social justice, but his writings on this great Victorian subject were neither penetrating nor sustained. Social relations, to Lewes, did not constitute the most critical aspect of social development; it was the spiritual, the moral, the "idealist" aspect that he considered most fundamental. Once a true philosophy—a true understanding of the relations of men and the universe—was achieved, all else would fall into place.

Those who come to the study of Lewes' work with the idea that he was primarily a literary critic are invariably struck by his "versatility." And they are forced into making of Lewes' criticism something more than it is. To judge him the most significant critic after Coleridge and before Arnold is, upon due consideration, a form of not so subtle derogation.[1] Victorian intellectual and cultural life encompassed more than literature and the arts; it required guidance in scientific and philosophical matters as well. The Victorians were

looking, above all, for an adequate world-view. Such a comprehension of the universe went beyond ordinary interest in
public affairs and literature, and incorporated a reinterpretation of the totality of human knowledge; it had to provide
intellectual assurance that such knowledge was true and
such an interpretation valid, and it had to be emotionally
satisfying, that is, complete. Lewes' philosophical interests
date from as early a period as his literary efforts, and it is
hard to resist the impression that potboiling was more
noticeable in the latter category than in the former. This is
not to say that Lewes wrote literary articles only to keep
himself alive while concentrating on philosophy. The success
of his career was due to his instinctive feel for what the public wanted and his ability to oblige them with semi-scientific
wisdom and philosophic *apercus* as well as usually lively
literary and dramatic criticism. And the priorities in his own
interests are only retrospectively apparent. But they are real.

There are many aspects of Lewes' construction of a
"meaningful cosmos" which are immediately recognizable
and readily appreciated in the modern context. Such are his
secular outlook, the materialistic — perhaps "naturalistic"
would be better — explanations he tried to find for very complex phenomena, the tempered empiricism, the appreciation for "wholes" and, not least of all, the very attempt to
come to terms with and to make sense of the entire universe
that humanity encounters. His positivistic enthusiasm, his
faith in science and the scientific method are perhaps too
extravagant for modern sensibilities; our sympathies are
more readily engaged by the mingling of faith and doubt of
Victorian thought as a whole. And, indeed, doubt was
present in Lewes' mind too, gnawing away at his attempts to
assert the certainty provided by the scientific method, and
at the completeness of its scope. The very extravagance of

his claims is easily read as the strained effort to put up a brave front; this too is something readily appreciated.

The versatility of Lewes' talents — for which John Gross tried to find a kinder name than dilettantism — is not, therefore, to be associated with the character of Will Ladislaw and the problem of a false vocation. Lewes was not a literary critic swamped by science and philosophy; nor was he a mere editor and the manager of George Eliot's genius who should have stayed within those safe confines. To be sure, he was much exercised over the problem of the false vocation as the analysis of the career of Percy Ranthorpe and the strident enunciation of the principle of sincerity indicated. But it would be more appropriate to say that Lewes' was not the problem of the false vocation so much as that of the impossible vocation. The comparison is to be made, not with Ladislaw, but with Casaubon; not with one who tried to be an artist though his talents lay elsewhere, but with the man who presumed to undertake

to show (what indeed had been attempted before, but not with that thoroughness, justice of comparison, and effectiveness of arrangement at which Mr. Casaubon aimed) that all the mythical systems or erratic mythical fragments in the world were corruptions of a tradition originally revealed. Having once mastered the true position and taken a firm footing there, the vast field of mythical constructions became intelligible, nay, luminous, with the reflected light of correspondences.

And it was Will Ladislaw who pointed out, to Dorothea's pain, that the subject chosen was "as changing as chemistry; new discoveries are making new points of view. Who," he asked, "wants a system on the basis of the four elements or a book to refute Paracelsus?"[2]

It does not require too much ingenuity to read in the mythical systems of Casaubon's studies the old metaphysics

and in the "tradition ·originally revealed" the new philosophy of reasoned realism. Of course, George Eliot did not
build the character of Casaubon around her beloved "hus-
band"; after all, she devoutly edited the last two volumes of
Problems for publication after Lewes' death. But can it be
that she did not, perhaps subconsciously, see the absurdity
and the hybris of the many nineteenth-century quests for
the key to the riddle of the universe? No doubt, it did not
occur to her that Lewes' effort might come under a similar
sentence; they both shared in the earnest concern for the reconstruction of the moral and intellectual world of thought
of their time. And Lewes was certainly unlike Casaubon in
character. His own attempt at philosophic restatement was
perhaps inconclusive, but he did not allow it to devour his
soul. It gave, instead, impetus to an innate intellectual
curiosity and to a more than intellectual passion — Plato
once called it *eros* — to master the many aspects of human
activity. Lewes' versatility was that of a lesser Goethe; his
writings therefore illuminate for us many areas of Victorian
thought. He entered into more of the diverse intellectual
interests of the Victorians than Bagehot, and with no less
earnestness though with far greater *brio* than Spencer. It
was impossible, Spencer said, to be dull in Lewes' company.
Wherever he went, as Eliza Lynn Linton remarked, "there
was a patch of intellectual sunshine."[3]

Appendix, Bibliographical Essay, Notes, Index

Appendix: Calendar of the Life of George Henry Lewes

1817   April 18: GHL was born in London.

1818   His father, John Lee Lewes, died.

                As a child, GHL lived for some time in Boulogne, France.

1825   His widowed mother (née Elizabeth Ashweek) married John Willim, Captain (retired) of the 18th Native Infantry Regiment in Bengal.

1828-
1830   At school in Brittany and Jersey.

1830-
1834   At school at Dr. Burney's in Greenwich.

                After this period of formal education, GHL continued his reading and began philosophical discussions while working for some time in a notary's office and then for a Russia merchant. He "walked the wards" for some time, and began his literary endeavors with a short story and a poem commended to Leigh Hunt's attention (1834).

1837   Lectured in philosophy at W. J. Fox's Chapel in Finsbury. He contributed to the *Monthly Repository,* formerly edited by

Fox, but now by R. H. Horne and Leigh Hunt. GHL's acquaintance with Dickens began after his review of *Pickwick* appeared.

1838-   In Germany with an introduction from Carlyle to Varnhagen
1839   von Ense.

1840   GHL's first major article, "French Drama," published in the
         Westminster Review. Friendship with J. S. Mill began.

1841   February 18: Married Agnes Jervis. He began to write for the
         Penny Cyclopaedia, a project of Charles Knight.

1842   Went to Paris for a month; there he met Auguste Comte and
         Victor Cousin.

         Began to write for the *Monthly Magazine* and the *British and
         Foreign Review.*

1843   Began to write for *Blackwood's,* the *Foreign Quarterly Review,* and the *Edinburgh Review.*

1844   Began to write for *Fraser's.*

1845   Visted Berlin; heard Schelling lecture.

         A Biographical History of Philosophy, 1st series, 2 volumes,
         published by Charles Knight.

1846   *A Biographical History of Philosophy,* 2nd series, also in two volumes, published by Charles Knight; also *The Spanish Drama: Lope de Vega and Calderon.*

1847   Visted France again.

Ranthorpe published by Chapman and Hall.

1848   *Rose, Blanche, and Violet* published by Smith, Elder.

The revolutions of 1848 stimulated GHL into preparing a life of Robespierre.

1849   *Life of Robespierre* published by Chapman and Hall.

February: Lectured on philosophy at the Mechanics' Institute in Liverpool.

March-April: Lectured at the Athenaeum in Manchester.

November: Lectured in Edinburgh.

In those three cities GHL performed in *The Merchant of Venice* and in his *Noble Heart.*

He made a trip to enlist support for a projected radical weekly, the *Free Speaker.*

Signs of a rift appeared in his marriage.

1850   March 30: first issue of a new weekly, renamed the *Leader,* which GHL edited with Thornton Hunt until the autumn of 1854.

1851   Apart from his duties at the *Leader* and writing various articles, GHL wrote more drama: "A Certain Age" and "The Game of Speculation."

Became acquainted with Herbert Spencer, through whom he met Marian Evans (GE). Spencer also rekindled his interest in science.

1852   Wrote various pieces for Charles Mathews on a more or less regular basis; this relationship continued until 1855.

1853   October 17: GE moved into her own apartment near Hyde Park. Haight dates her intimacy with GHL from this move.

1854   July 20: GHL left with GE for Germany.

1855   March: They returned to England. GHL spent a few weeks straightening out his affairs. They lived in various temporary accommodations until October 3, when they settled at 8 Park Shot, Richmond.

Life and Works of Goethe published in two volumes by David Nutt.

1856   May-June: With GE in Ilfracombe and Tenby for research published in *Blackwood's* as "Sea-side Studies." GHL's connection with this publishing house was most fortunate. In November he forwarded GE's "Amos Barton," which, like almost everything she wrote subsequently, was published by William Blackwood and Sons.

1857   March-July: With GE to Jersey and the Scilly Isles for more sea-side studies.

1858   (GE finished *Adam Bede*).

1859   February 5: The "Leweses" moved to Holly Lodge, South
            Fields, Wandsworth, where they became acquainted with
            the Richard Congreves, their neighbors.

1860   March-June: With GE to Italy and Switzerland. (GE, *Mill on
            the Floss.*)

1861   April-June: With GE to Italy. (GE, *Silas Marner;* working on
            Romola.)

1862   Consulting editor of *Cornhill* (until October 1864).

1863   The Leweses bought the Priory, 21 North Bank, Regents
            Park. (*Romola* was published in *Cornhill.*)

1864   *Aristotle* published by Smith, Elder. GHL's stepfather died.

1865   Holiday in Paris to arrange for articles from Eugène Four-
            cade (editor of the *Revue des deux Mondes*) for *Pall Mall Ga-
            zette,* for which GHL was now adviser.

            Under pressure from an old friend, Anthony Trollope, GHL
            also became editor of the *Fortnightly Review.* "Principles of
            Success in Literature" in the *Fortnightly Review* (May 15 to
            November 1).

1866   January: Resigned as adviser to *PMG.*

December: Resigned from the *Fortnightly* because of ill health.

1867   October: GHL and Spencer, on a walking trip, met Mrs. Cross in Weybridge.

December: Beginning preparations for *Problems of Life and Mind,* GHL consulted physiologists in Bonn and Heidelberg.

1868   April, June, July, November: Articles on Darwin in *FR*.

GHL went to Oxford at Dr. H. W. Acland's invitation to attend the meeting of the British Medical Association.

1869   March-April: With GE to Italy, where they met John Cross for the first time.

1870   December 10: GHL's mother died.

1872   (*Middlemarch* published.)

1874   *Problems of Life and Mind,* first series: *The Foundations of a Creed* in two volumes published by Trübner (1874-1875).

1876   March 31: Physiological Society founded with GHL a founder-member.

Summer: With GE in France and Switzerland, returning to London as the last book of *Daniel Deronda* was published. In December, they bought a country house at Witley, near the Crosses, the Tennysons, and the son of Sir Henry Holland who was their physician and an old friend.

1877   *The Physical Basis of Mind,* the third volume, constituting
            the second series, of *Problems,* published. Volumes four and
            five, constituting the third series of *Problems,* were published
            posthumously in 1879 as *The Study of Psychology* and *Mind
            as a Function of the Organism,* respectively.

1878   November 14: GHL became violently ill, and died on No-
            vember 30.

Bibliographical Essay

Most of Lewes' manuscripts are at the Beinecke Rare Book and Manuscript Library, Yale University. In addition to most of his extant letters, the collection includes drafts for *Problems* and "Principles"; his journal in three volumes numbered X, XI and XII, and covering the period from July 24, 1856, to May 6, 1870; eight volumes of his diary covering the years 1869 to 1877, inclusive; and various notebooks containing aphorisms or historical outlines. At the Berg Collection of the New York Public Library are seven letters from Lewes to Thornton Hunt regarding the founding of the *Leader* (there are also a few to Lewes from the Rev. Edmund Larken); a prospectus for the *Leader*, then to be called the "Free Speaker"; and Lewes' Literary Receipts Book which has been published in volume seven of *The George Eliot Letters* edited by Gordon S. Haight. The Archives Positivistes (Musée d'Auguste Comte), Paris, has ten of Lewes' letters to Comte and eleven from Comte to Lewes. A few of Lewes' earliest letters are to be found in the Correspondence of Leigh Hunt at the British Museum (Add. MSS. 38,523).

I have read with pleasure and profit Robert Bernard Doremus' "George Henry Lewes: A Descriptive Biography, with Especial Attention to His Interest in the Theatre" (2 vols., Ph.D. dissertation, Harvard University, 1940). Allan R. Brick's "The 'Leader': Organ of Radicalism" (Ph.D. dissertation, Yale University, 1957) gives a useful account of the founding of this lively weekly. James Maurice Murphy's "Positivism in England: The Reception of Comte's Doctrines, 1840-1870" (Ph.D. dissertation, Columbia University, 1968) is perfunctory but led me to the interesting letters in the Archives Positivistes. I found Stephen Michael Fishman's "Epistemology of G. H. Lewes" (Ph.D. dissertation, Columbia University, 1967) too technical for my needs and comprehension.

On the profession of letters, John Gross's *Rise and Fall of the Man of Letters* (London, Weidenfeld and Nicolson, 1969) is particularly useful. Lewes' literary criticism (and other aspects of his thought) has been indifferently treated by Alice R. Kaminsky, *George Henry Lewes as Literary Critic* (Syracuse University Press, 1968), and by Edgar W. Hirshberg, *George Henry Lewes* (New York, Twayne Publishers, 1970). Kaminsky's bibliography of Lewes' works is, however, the fullest in print; although it contains some inaccuracies, it is more convenient to use than the otherwise indispensable *Wellesley Index;* in addition she provides a useful list of articles on Lewes. In *The Literary Criticism of George Henry Lewes* (Lincoln, University of Nebraska Press, 1965), Kaminsky has compiled extracts from Lewes' writings.

"The Principles of Success in Literature," which Lewes first published in 1865, has been reprinted a few times, most recently with an introduction by Geoffrey Tillotson (Farnborough, Gregg, 1969). Lewes' *On Actors and the Art of Acting* (1875; reprint Grove Press, 1957) consists of articles published in the *Pall Mall Gazette* in 1865; it is still well worth the while to search out the old files of the *Pall Mall Gazette* for the years 1865 and 1866 when Lewes' articles, signed "L," sometimes appeared three or four times a week. His dramatic criticisms in the *Leader* (1850-1854) appeared with the pen-name "Vivian"; they too are voluminous and, though not as polished as the *PMG* pieces, are as full of "fun" and sharp observations. Also interesting and readable is *The Spanish Drama: Lope de Vega and Calderon* (1846). Apart from these, his *Life and Works of Goethe* has significance for those interested in Lewes' criticism; the third edition is available in Everyman's Library. This work also throws light on his general attitudes towards science and philosophy; it is especially useful since his *Biographical History of Philosophy* (1845-1846; 2nd ed., 1857; 3rd ed., 1867) has not been reprinted. Lewes' articles on Darwin, Spinoza, and Comte, and "On the Dread and Dislike of Science," in the *Fortnightly Review* are well worth reading. The *Sea-side Studies* (1858), originally articles in *Blackwood's*, and the *Studies in Animal Life* (1862), which first appeared as articles in the *Cornhill Magazine*, are delightful examples of Victorian "zoologizing." His *Aristotle: A Chapter in the History of Science* (1864) contains some important statements on method in science and philosophy. The five volumes of *Problems of Life and Mind* (1874-1879), alas, were correctly described by Gross as "research fodder"; they also had a complex publication history. The first and second volumes constituted the first series, entitled *The Foundations of a Creed;* the third volume by itself constituted the second series, entitled *The Physical Basis of Mind;* the fourth and fifth volumes, published posthumously as the third series, treated four "problems": *Problem the First* in volume four, with its subtitle, *The Study of Psychology: Its Object, Scope, and Method:* and the other three problems in volume five. (This work is referred to in the notes as *Problems*, volumes I through V.) Jack Kaminsky's "Empirical Metaphysics of George Henry Lewes" (*Journal of the History of Ideas*, 13 [1952], 314-332) is a straight-forward account of the subject.

It goes without saying that I have found Professor Gordon S. Haight's biography of George Eliot and his edition of her letters indispensable; I only regret not having been able to use the supplementary volume of the Letters. For the rest, I hope the notes provide adequate bibliographical references.

Notes

Abbreviations

BFR	*British and Foreign Review*
Blackwood's	*Blackwood's Edinburgh Magazine*
BQR	*British Quarterly Review*
Cornhill	*Cornhill Magazine*
ER	*Edinburgh Review*
FQR	*Foreign Quarterly Review*
FR	*Fortnightly Review*
Fraser's	*Fraser's Magazine*
PMG	*Pall Mall Gazette*
PMLA	*Publications of the Modern Language Association*
SR	*Saturday Review*
VS	*Victorian Studies*
WR	*Westminster Review*

1: The Making of the Man of Letters

1. Noel Annan, "The Intellectual Aristocracy," in *Studies in Social History: A Tribute to G. M. Trevelyan,* ed. J. H. Plumb (London, Longmans, 1955), ch. 8; Stephen: *DNB*, "George Henry Lewes."

2. GHL, *The Life and Works of Goethe* (2 vols., London, 1855), I, 20. All references are to this edition unless otherwise specified.

3. Richard D. Altick, "The Sociology of Authorship," *Bulletin of the New York Public Library,* 66 (1962), 389-404.

4. Samuel Smiles, *Autobiography,* ed. Thomas Mackay (New York, E. P. Dutton and Company, 1905), 26.

5. G. F. Barwick, "The Magazines of the Nineteenth Century," *Transactions of the Bibliographical Society,* 9 (1909-1911), 238. For the *Newspaper Press Directory,* see Alvar Ellegård, "The Readership of the

Periodical Press in Mid-Victorian Britain," *Acta Universitatis Gothoburgensis,* 63 (1957), no. 3, p. 4; Dickens: Charles Knight, *Passages from the Life of Charles Knight* (Boston, 1874), 426f.

6. See Michael Wolff, "Victorian Reviewers and Cultural Responsibility," in *1859: Entering An Age of Crisis,* ed. P. Appleman, et al. (Bloomington, Indiana, University of Indiana Press, 1959), 269-289. Cf. John Cross, *The Rise and Fall of the Man of Letters* (London, Weidenfeld and Nicolson, 1969), 87f.

7. Charles Lee Lewes, *Memoirs,* ed. John Lee Lewes (4 vols., London, 1805), I, 9-13.

8. Anna T. Kitchel, *George Lewes and George Eliot: A Review of Records* (New York, J. Day, 1933), 7; Charles Lee Lewes, *Comic Sketches* (London, 1804), Introduction, xxiv; *The George Eliot Letters,* ed. Gordon S. Haight (7 vols., New Haven, Yale University Press, 1954-1955), II, 216, n.3; III, 372, n.2; VII, 365f.

9. *Autobiographical Notes of William Bell Scott,* ed. W. Minto (2 vols., London, 1892; reprint New York, AMS, 1970), I, 130n.

10. Frederick Locker-Lampson, *My Confidences* (London, 1869), 114-118; *Athenaeum,* no. 2667 (December 7, 1878), 726: anonymous obituary notice of GHL.

11. Altick, "Sociology," 395; Thomas S. Bayne, "An Evening with Carlyle," *Athenaeum,* no. 3101 (April 2, 1887), 450; *The Life and Letters of Benjamin Jowett,* ed. Evelyn Abbott and Lewis Campbell (2nd ed., 2 vols., London, 1897), I, 261, and cf. I, 130f.

12. Huxley's review: *WR,* n.s. 5: 255f. (Jan. 1854); Lewes' signed response: *Leader,* 5: 40 (Jan. 14, 1854).

13. GHL, "Journal," Jan. 25, 1859, cited in Gordon S. Haight, *George Eliot, A Biography* (New York, Oxford University Press, 1968), 271f. Lewes claimed that in 1836 he studied medicine for a while and had the inspiring thought of writing a "treatise on the Philosophy of the Mind in which the doctrines of Reid, Stewart, and Brown were to be physiologically interpreted" (*Problems,* I, v).

14. See GHL to Leigh Hunt, Oct. 2, 1834, Nov. 15, 1838, and Apr. 10, 1840, in "Correspondence of J. H. Leigh Hunt," supplementary volume I, 1807-1844 (Add. MSS. 38,523, BM). For Hunt, see Edmund Blunden, *Leigh Hunt, A Biography* (London, Cobden-Sanderson, 1930), 276. For the *Monthly Repository* and Fox, see Francis E. Mineka, *The Dissidence of Dissent: The Monthly Repository, 1806-1838* (Chapel Hill, University of North Carolina Press, 1944).

In his "Journal" (Feb. 27, 1859), however, Lewes referred to Hunt's *Autobiography* as "intensely coxcombical and feeble." The entry for

March 2 mused upon the strangeness of outliving one's youthful adulation.

15. Mill to Napier, Feb. 18, 1842, in *The Earlier Letters of John Stuart Mill, 1812-1848*, ed. Francis E. Mineka (2 vols., Toronto, University of Toronto Press, 1963), II, 499.

16. Mill to Comte, July 13, 1843, in *ibid.,* 591.

17. GE, *Letters*, IV, 333.

18. Haight, *George Eliot,* 169; GE, *Letters,* II, 176f.; Mill, *The Earlier Letters,* II, 449, 557f.

19. Francis Espinasse, *Literary Recollections and Sketches* (London, 1893), 279, 281. A copy of the novel with Carlyle's bookplate and inscribed to "Giovanina Carlyle, with kindest regards from G. H. Lewes" is in the Berg Collection, NYPL. The annotations in it are in Carlyle's characteristically neat hand.

20. Espinasse, *Literary Recollections,* 59.

21. R. H. Hutton, for instance, wrote of the "limpness and want of concentration in Goethe's whole nature intellectual and moral" ("Goethe and His Influence," *Essays Theological and Literary* [2 vols., London, 1880], II, 9). Lewes' "Character and Works of Goethe" appeared in *BFR,* 14 (1843), 78-135.

22. *The Memoirs of Margaret Fuller Ossoli,* ed. J. F. Clarke, R. W. Emerson, and W. H. Channing (2 vols., Boston, 1852), II, 186; Espinasse, *Literary Recollections,* 279f. 282.

23. For Lockhart, see Walter Graham, *Tory Criticism in the Quarterly Review: 1809-1853* (New York, Columbia University Press, 1921), 22; for Lewes' appraisal of Hunt: *Leader,* 1:328 (June 29, 1850).

24. Haight, *George Eliot,* 130; cf. Alice R. Kaminsky, *George Henry Lewes as Literary Critic* (Syracuse, Syracuse University Press, 1968), 3f.

25. For Thackeray, see Hugh Walker, *Literature of the Victorian Era* (Cambridge, University Press, 1921), 179; for Mrs. Carlyle: *Jane Welsh Carlyle: Letters to Her Family 1839-1863,* ed. Leonard Huxley (London, John Murray, 1924), 319f.

26. On Spinoza, see *A Biographical History of Philosophy,* III (London, 1846), 147, and "Spinoza," *FR,* 4 (1866), 395-406; on his relations with Smith: *The Story of William and Lucy Smith,* ed. George S. Merriam (Boston, 1895), 61.

27. Scott, *Autobiographical Notes,* I, 129-131.

28. "Communism as an Ideal: Social Reform," *Leader,* 1:733f. (Oct. 26, 1850); "The Apprenticeship of Life," *ibid.,* 42 and 90 (April 6 and Sept. 14, 1850); letter to Masson, *ibid.,* 469-470 (Aug. 10, 1850).

29. Arnott: GE, *Letters,* II, 126; Alice Helps: *ibid.,* 422, n. 2.

30. David Masson, *Memories of London in the Forties* (London, W. Blackwood and Sons, 1908), 211, 222; Leonard Huxley, *The House of Smith, Elder* (London, Printed for private circulation, 1923), 35, 39, 46. For the Fielding Club, see Edmund Yates, *Edmund Yates: His Recollections and Experiences* (2 vols., London, 1884), I, 235-242.

31. Espinasse, *Literary Recollections,* 230.

32. John Morley, *Recollections* (2 vols., New York, Macmillan, 1917), I, 371. Cf. Haight, *George Eliot,* 388f.

33. Barnes: A. Aspinall, "The Social Status of Journalists at the Beginning of the Nineteenth Century," *Review of English Studies,* 21 (1945), 230; Hutton and the *Spectator:* "Richard Holt Hutton," *Academy,* 52 (1897), 221; first issue of the *Leader* (March 30, 1850), 22; Holyoake, *Sixty Years of an Agitator's Life* (2 vols., London, 1892), I, 239.

34. Lewes to M. Napier, Nov. 7, 1842, in *Selections from the Correspondence of Macvey Napier, Esq.,* ed. M. Napier (London, 1879), 413.

35. Lewes to T. Hunt, [1849] (ALS, Berg Collection, NYPL).

36. GE, *Letters,* I, 357, and II, 46f.

37. Herbert Spencer, *An Autobiography* (2 vols., New York, D. Appleton and Company, 1904), I, 467.

38. *Leader,* 1:860 (Nov. 30, 1850).

39. George Bernard Shaw, *Our Theatre in the Nineties* (3 vols., London, Constable, 1932), II, 162.

40. J. W. Robertson Scott, *The Story of the Pall Mall Gazette* (London, Oxford University Press, 1950), 148.

41. Kitchel, *George Lewes,* 46; Espinasse, *Literary Recollections,* 283.

42. Frederic Harrison, "G. H. Lewes," *Academy,* 14: 543f. (Dec. 7, 1878).

43. *The Life of Maximilien Robespierre* (London, 1849), viii; *Life and Works of Goethe* (Everyman's ed., London, 1965), Introduction, viii.

44. Max Weber, "The Social Psychology of World Religions," in *From Max Weber,* ed. H. H. Gerth and C. Wright Mills (New York, Oxford University Press, 1946), 281.

45. *Jane Welsh Carlyle: Letters,* 329.

46. For Smith, see Scott, *Pall Mall Gazette,* 71; for Lewes: "Thoughts for the Thoughtful" (MS, n.d., Beinecke Library); Justin McCarthy, " 'George Eliot' and George Lewes," *Galaxy,* 7:808f. (June 1869).

47. C. S. Peel, "Homes and Habits," in *Early Victorian England,* ed. G. M. Young (2 vols., London, Oxford University Press, 1934), I, 104, 107f., and 126f.; cf. Thomas Webster, *Encyclopedia for Domestic Economy* (London, 1852), 330f.

48. Haight, *George Eliot,* 132.

49. For Sibyl, see G. M. Young, "The Greatest Victorian," in *Victor-*

ian Essays (London, Oxford University Press, 1962), 124, and cf. 132; for the phrase "marmoreal image," Haight's edition of John Chapman's diaries, *George Eliot and John Chapman* (Hamden, Conn., 2nd edition, Archon Books, 1969), Preface. For the "majestic arm," see Oscar Browning, *Memories of Sixty Years at Eton, Cambridge, and Elsewhere* (London, John Lane, 1910), 111, 192; for observations on Lewes, see Scott, *Pall Mall Gazette,* 71, and M. Betham-Edwards, *Mid-Victorian Memories* (London, John Murray, 1919), 44.

50. See Walter Graham, *English Literary Periodicals* (New York, T. Nelson and Sons, 1930), 258, 304.

51. Darwin: GHL to Sir Henry Acland, Nov. 1868 (ALS, Beinecke Library); Grant-Duff: see his *Notes from a Diary, 1873-1881* (2 vols., London, 1898), II, 88.

2: *The Man of Letters as Moralist*

1. Basil Willey, *The Eighteenth-Century Background* (London, Chatto and Windus, 1940), Preface; G. Kitson Clark, *The Making of Victorian England* (Cambridge, Mass., Harvard University Press, 1962), 126; cf. G. M. Young, *Victorian Essays* (Oxford University Press, 1962), 57.

2. R. H. Hutton, *Essays Theological and Literary* (2 vols., London, 1880), I, 33. The views of the noted Unitarian theologian, James Martineau, were similar: see A. W. Jackson, *James Martineau* (Boston, 1900), 399f., 423f.; Owen Chadwick, *The Victorian Church,* I (London, A. and C. Black, 1966), 528f.; Howard Murphy, "The Ethical Revolt against Christian Orthodoxy in Early Victorian England," *American Historical Review,* 60 (1955), 800-817.

3. R. H. Hutton, *Aspects of Religious and Scientific Thought,* ed. E. M. Roscoe (London, 1880), 15; GHL, "Literature," *Leader,* 2:442 (May 10, 1851), and 1:185 (May 18, 1850).

4. ALS to Dr. Weir Mitchell, Aug. 30, 1852 (MS, Beinecke Library); "Men of Thought and Men of Action," *Douglas Jerrold's Shilling Magazine,* 7:528-532 (June 1848).

5. "Percy Bysshe Shelley," *WR,* 35:318 (April 1841); "Recent Tragedies," *WR,* 37:342 (April 1842).

6. "Shelley," 321, 307.

7. "The Revolutionary Firebrand," *Douglas Jerrold's Shilling Magazine,* 5:327, 329 (April 1847).

8. *Leader,* 2:345 (April 12, 1851).

9. F. D. Maurice, *Moral and Metaphysical Philosophy* (2 vols., Lon-

don, 1872), II, 675; A. Bain, *John Stuart Mill* (London, 1882), 75.

10. GHL, "Comte and Mill," *FR*, 6: 406 (Oct. 1, 1866); A. Comte, *Cours de philosophie positive*, I, 40f., cited in D. G. Charlton, *Positivist Thought in France during the Second Empire* (Oxford, Clarendon Press, 1959), 38; GHL, "The Modern Metaphysics and Moral Philosophy of France," *BFR*, 15 (1843), 353.

11. "The Coming Reformation," in four parts, *Douglas Jerrold's Shilling Magazine*, 5: 436-448, 509-519 (May, June 1847); 6: 35-45, 168-176 (July, Aug. 1847).

12. "The Duodecimo Statesman," *Leader*, 1:332 (June 29, 1850).

13. "The Coming Reformation," *Douglas Jerrold's Shilling Magazine*, 6:41 (July 1847).

14. G. J. Holyoake, *Sixty Years of an Agitator's Life* (2 vols., London, 1892), I, 240.

15. "Roman History," *FQR*, 34 (1844-1845), 450f.

16. "Modern Metaphysics," *BFR*, 15 (1843), 402.

17. "Modern French Historians," *WR*, 36: 276 (Oct. 1841); "History by Modern Frenchmen." *BQR*, 14 (1851), 407.

18. Arthur O. Lovejoy, *The Great Chain of Being* (Cambridge, Mass., Harvard University Press, 1936), 294.

19. J. S. Mill, *The Positive Philosophy of Auguste Comte* (London, 1861; Boston, 1866), 79-80.

20. This was a serious question for the Victorians; see J. W. Burrow, *Evolution and Society* (London, Cambridge University Press, 1966), 205; also Isaiah Berlin's "John Stuart Mill and the Ends of Life," in his *Four Essays on Liberty* (London and New York, Oxford University Press, 1969).

21. "State of Historical Science in France," *BFR*, 16 (1844), 85; "Buchez and Danou on the Science of History," *FQR*, 32:329 (Jan. 1844); "Contemporary Literature of France," *WR*, 58:617 (Oct. 1852).

22. "History by Modern Frenchmen," *BQR*, 14 (1851), 410.

23. J. W. Bury, *The Idea of Progress* (London, Macmillan, 1932), 4. Cf. Burrow, *Evolution and Society*, 264, and Young, *Victorian Essays*, 135.

24. "Uncivilised Man," *Blackwood's*, 89 (1861), 41: "Modern Metaphysics," *BFR*, 15 (1843), 355; "State of Historical Science," *BFR*, 16 (1844), 81.

25. "The Art of History—Macaulay," *BQR*, 23 (1856), 307, 302f., 306.

26. "The Thirty Years' Peace," *BQR*, 11 (1850), 365; "American Books," *Leader*, 1:16 (Mar. 30, 1850).

27. "Thirty Years' Peace," 360-364.

28. *Ibid.*, 366.

29. E. Halévy, *Victorian Years*, vol. 4 of *A History of the English People in the Nineteenth Century* (London, Ernest Benn, 1951), 252-265; S. H. Beer, *British Politics in the Collectivist Age* (New York, Knopf, 1965), ch. 3.

30. GHL, "The Free Speaker" (MS holograph, Berg Collection). This was never published. Parts of Hunt's prospectus appeared in Holyoake, *Sixty Years*, I, 236; and in Francis Espinasse, *Literary Recollections and Sketches* (London, 1893), 236.

31. Cited in Holyoake, *Sixty Years*, I, 236.

32. *Leader*, 1:613f. (Sept. 21, 1850).

33. "Thirty Years' Peace," *BQR*, 11 (1850), 366f.; *Leader*, 1:204 (May 25, 1850).

34. *Ibid.*, 1:134 and 36 (May 4 and April 6, 1850).

35. "Communism as an Ideal," *ibid.*, 1:733 (Oct. 26, 1850); review of Massey's poem in *ibid.*, 2:417 (May 3, 1851).

36. "Memoir of Bulwer," *Bentley's Miscellany*, 24:2 (July 1848); "Macaulay's *History of England*," BQR, 9 (1849), 35.

37. *Leader*, 1:663 (Oct. 5, 1850); "Journal," Feb. 17, 1859.

38. "Mrs. Grundy and the Public Press," *Leader*, 1:36 (Apr. 6, 1850). Cf. Oscar Maurer, "My Squeamish Public: Some Problems of Victorian Magazine Publishers and Editors," in *Studies in Bibliography* 12 (1959), 21-40. On Newman's *Phases*, see *Leader*, 1:279 (June 15, 1850), and William Robbins, *The Newman Brothers* (Cambridge, Mass., Harvard University Press, 1966), 112-114.

39. "Michelet on Auricular Confession and Direction," *FQR*, 35 (1845), 197; Halévy, *Victorian Years*, 368; Owen Chadwick, *Victorian Miniature* (London, Hodder and Stoughton, 1960), 14; E. P. Thompson, *The Making of the English Working Classes* (London, V. Gollancz, 1963), 71-73.

40. *Leader*, 1:850 (Nov. 30, 1850), and 2:38f. (Jan. 11, 1851). Cf. Halévy, *Victorian Years*, 313f., 368f.

41. Berlin, *Four Essays*, 193, 187; "Communism as an Ideal," *Leader*, 1:733f. (Oct. 26, 1850).

42. GHL, review of Southwood Smith's *The Philosophy of Health* in *SR*, 19:148 (Feb. 4, 1865); "A Pleasant French Book," *Blackwood's*, 84:682f. (Dec. 1858).

43. GHL, review of Spencer's *Social Statics* in *Leader*, 2:248-250 (March 15, 1851).

44. GHL's review in *SR*, 1: 164f., 237f. (Jan. 12 and 26, 1856).

45. H. Spencer, *Social Statics* (London, 1851), chs. 9 and 10.

46. Holyoake, *Sixty Years*, I, 239; Royden J. Harrison, *Before the Socialists: Studies in Labour and Politics, 1861-1881* (London, Routledge and K. Paul, 1965), ch. 6.

47. "Farewell Causerie," *FR*, 6:892 (Dec. 1, 1866); "Communism as an Ideal," *Leader*, 1:734 (Oct. 26, 1850).

48. *Leader*, 1: 182f. (May 18, 1850), 130 (May 4, 1850), and 837 (Nov. 23, 1850). Cf. *ibid.*, 4:183 (Feb. 19, 1853).

49. H. Spencer, *An Autobiography* (2 vols., New York, D. Appleton and Company, 1904), II, 237.

50. "Guizot's *Democracy in France*," *Athenaeum*, no. 1108 (Jan. 20, 1849), 68; "History by Modern Frenchmen," *BQR*, 14:417 (Nov. 1851); "Professor Owen and the Science of Life," *Fraser's*, 53:79 (Jan. 1856).

51. "Causeries," *FR*, 4:508f. (April 1, 1866). See J. Roach, "Liberalism and the Victorian Intelligentsia," *Cambridge Historical Journal*, 13 (1957), 58-81, for the disenchantment with liberalism.

52. H. Taine, *History of English Literature*, trans. H. van Laun (4 vols., Edinburgh, 1874), IV, 144; A. Trollope, *Autobiography*, ed. Bradford A. Booth (Berkeley, University of California Press, 1947), 186.

53. "George Sand," *Monthly Magazine*, 95:578, 582 (June 1842); preface to *Rose, Blanche, and Violet* (London, 1848).

54. "Balzac and George Sand," *FQR*, 33:265, 269f. (July 1844); "The Lady Novelists," *WR*, 58:140 (July 1852); "Ruth and Villette," *WR*, 59:475f. (April 1853); "Currer Bell's '*Shirley*,' " *ER*, 91 (1850), 163f.

55. "A Word to Young Authors on Their True Position," *Hood's Magazine*, 3:366, 369f. (April 1845); cf. "The Principles of Success in Literature," pt. 1, *FR*, 1:87 (May 15, 1865); "Forster's Life of Goldsmith," *BQR*, 8:9-11 (Aug. 1848); "Eugène Sue: *Les Mystères de Paris*," *BFR*, 18 (1844), 217f., 238; "Charles Paul de Kock," *Monthly Magazine*, 95:136f., 142 (Feb. 1842); and review of *La Tulipe noire* in *Leader*, 1:716 (Oct. 19, 1850).

56. "Robert Buchanan," *FR*, 1:443-445 (July 1, 1865).

57. "Antigone," *Leader*, 1:137f. (May 4, 1850), "Currer Bell's '*Shirley*,' " *ER*, 91 (1850), 160; "The Novels of Jane Austen," *Blackwood's*, 86 (1859), 108.

58. "Hegel's Aesthetics: Philosophy of Art"; the quotations in this paragraph and the next are taken from *BFR*, 13 (1842), 1-49.

59. GHL, *The Spanish Drama* (London, 1846), 176; "A. W. Schlegel," *FQR*, 32:163 (Oct. 1843); *Life of Goethe*, II, 433f. René Wellek (*A History of Modern Criticism* [4 vols., New Haven, Yale University Press, 1955-1965] II, 327) sees in Hegel's remark "a subtle distinction" between the "*Philister* who consume imported goods" and the "figures of an epic and heroic setting, closed in itself, consuming the local product."

60. "Lessing," *ER*, 82:451-453 (Oct. 1845).

61. On Hegel, see Wellek, *History of Modern Criticism*, II, 318-334, and III, 213, and K. Lowith, *From Hegel to Nietzsche*, trans. David E.

Green (London, Constable, 1965; from 3rd revised German edition), 5-8. On Lessing, see Ernst Cassirer, *The Philosophy of the Enlightenment*, trans. Fritz C. A. Koelln and James P. Pettegrove (Princeton University Press, 1951), 348, 357-360.

62. "Literature," *Leader*, 1:62 (April 13, 1850); and cf. *ibid.*, 183 and 566 (May 8 and Sept. 7, 1850).

63. "The Principles of Success" was first published in 1865 in six issues of *FR:* 1:85-95 (May 15), 185-196 (June 1), 572-589 (July 15), 697-709 (Aug. 1); 2:257-268 (Sept. 15), 689-710 (Nov. 1).

64. "Victor Hugo's New Novel," FR, 5:30, 32-43, 46 (May 15, 1866); "The New Classic Drama in France," *FQR*, 36:33-37 (Oct. 1845); "Balzac and George Sand," *FQR*, 33:281 (July 1844).

65. *Selections from the Correspondence of Macvey Napier, Esq.*, ed. M. Napier (London, 1879), 446f.; "Causeries," *FR*, 6:760 (Nov. 1, 1866); "Shakespeare's Critics: English and Foreign," *ER*, 90:46, 54f. (July 1849).

66. "Realism in Art: Recent German Fiction," *WR*, 70:493 (Oct. 1858); "Glimpses and Guesses" (MS, Beinecke Library), 26; "Principles of Success," *FR*, 1: 187, 588f., 578.

67. "Dramatic Reform," *ER*, 78:387 (Oct. 1843).

68. "Stafford and the Historical Drama," *WR*, 41:119, 121 (March 1844); cf. James C. Simmons, "The Novelist as Historian," *VS*, 14 (1971), 293-305; "Lynn's Amymone," *Athenaeum*, no. 1087 (Aug. 26, 1848), 853; "Historical Romance—Alexandre Dumas," *BQR*, 7:191, 193 (Feb. 1848).

69. "The Character and Works of Goethe," *BFR*, 14 (1843), 78f., 91, 111.

70. *Life of Goethe*, II, 388, 76, 212; cf. "Character and Works," 109.

71. *Life of Goethe*, 3rd ed. (London, 1875), 51; cf. the first edition, I, 72.

72. *Life of Goethe*, II, 215; I, 75. Lewes thought, however, that the dangers of Schiller's influence were more than offset by the positive good of its having inspired Goethe to great poetical works such as *Hermann und Dorothea*.

73. *Life of Goethe*, II, 234f., 236f., 203-210. Lewes was apparently referring to *Wilhelm Meisters Lehrjahre*.

74. *Life of Goethe*, II, 283; "Shakespeare's Critics," *ER*, 90:68 (July 1849).

75. *Life of Goethe*, II, 280-282, 319f. This philosophical explication of the legend was first offered in "The Three Fausts," *BFR*, 18 (1844), 66.

76. *Life of Goethe*, II, 279. Of his own age, Lewes had once complained that great art was impossible, for great subjects were no longer available ("Robert Browning and the Poetry of the Age," BQR, 6:492f. [Nov. 1847]).

77. Cf. "A Word to Young Authors," *Hood's Magazine*, 3:366 (April 1845). Quotations from "Principles" are not separately noted.

78. "The Novels of Jane Austen," *Blackwood's*, 86 (1859), 99-113, and "Principles," *FR*, 1:579.

79. "Recent Novels, French and English," *Fraser's*, 36:691 (Dec. 1847).

80. "Life in Central Africa," *Blackwood's*, 89:440 (April 1861).

81. "The Life and Works of Leopardi," *Fraser's*, 38:664 (Dec. 1848); "Alfieri and the Italian Drama," *BFR*, 17 (1844), 366.

82. Sincerity was the "new cant word of the criticism of the time, as if conviction, sincerity could assure good art" (Wellek, *History of Modern Criticism*, III, 87); cf. Patricia M. Ball, "Sincerity: The Rise and Fall of a Critical Term," *Modern Language Review*, 59 (1964), 1-11.

83. *From Wax Weber,* ed. H. H. Gerth and C. Wright Mills (New York, Oxford University Press, 1946), 271.

84. *The Spanish Drama,* 87.

85. *Life of Goethe,* II, 314.

86. *Problems,* I, 174.

87. "Journal," Feb. 12, 1859, in Eliot, *Letters*, III, 12.

88. *Biographical History,* III, 217; "Shakespeare's Critics," *ER,* 90 (1849), 40; *Comte's Philosophy,* 281; "Causeries," *FR,* 6:760 (Nov. 1, 1866). In "The Concept of Evolution in Literary History," René Wellek has made an inconclusive attempt to elucidate the problems of coming to terms with that idea (in M. Halle, ed., *For Roman Jakobson* [The Hague, 1950], 653-661).

89. "A Word about Tom Jones," *Blackwood's,* 87:331f. (March 1860); "Principles," *FR,* 1:89.

90. *FR,* n.s. 11: 141-154 (Feb. 1872). Cf. G. S. Haight, "Dickens and Lewes," *PMLA,* 71 (1956), 166-168.

91. For Lewes' difficulties with Balzac, see "Balzac," *Monthly Magazine,* 91 (1842), 463-472; "Balzac and George Sand," *FQR,* 33 (1844), 265-298.

92. "Dickens in Relation to Criticism," *FR,* n.s. 11:151, 142.

3: The Construction of a Victorian World-View

1. Charles Coulston Gillispie, *Genesis and Geology* (Cambridge, Mass., Harvard University Press, 1951) provides a fascinating analysis of the controversy over new geological theories, Alvar Ellegård for that over the *Origin* in *Darwin and the General Reader* (Göteborg, 1958). cf.

Walter F. Cannon, "John Herschel and the Idea of Science," *Journal of the History of Ideas,* 22 (1961), 215-239, and "The Normative Role of Science in Early Victorian Thought," *ibid.,* 25 (1964), 487-502.

2. R. K. Webb, *Harriet Martineau, A Radical Victorian* (New York, Columbia University Press, 1950), xi.

3. GHL, "Journal," Jan. 10, 1868, and Oct. 27, 1859. Lewes also wrote, sometimes in collaboration with John Herschel the astronomer, for the column "Notes on Science" in the *Cornhill.*

4. *Leader,* 4:64 (Jan. 15, 1853); GHL, "Seeing Is Believing," *Blackwood's,* 88 (1860), 381.

5. *Studies in Animal Life* (London, 1862), 74; "Philosophy as an Element of Culture," *Universal Review* (March 1859), 269-271, 275.

6. *Sea-side Studies* (London, 1858), viii; *Animal Life,* 9f., 36.

7. George Eliot, *Letters,* ed. Gordon S. Haight (7 vols., New Haven, Yale University Press, 1954-1955), III, 177, 189; J. M. Forrester, "Who Put the George in George Eliot?," *British Medical Journal,* 1 (1970), 166. Cf. R. E. Smith, "George Henry Lewes and His 'Physiology of Common Life', 1859," *Proceedings of the Royal Society of Medicine,* 53 (1960), 569-574.

8. "Mr. Darwin's Hypotheses" appeared in four issues of the *FR:* n.s. 3:353-373 (April 1, 1868), and 611-628 (June 1, 1868); n.s. 4: 61-80 (July 1, 1868), and 492-509 (Nov. 1, 1868).

9. A. Dwight Culler, "The Darwinian Revolution," in *The Art of Victorian Prose,* ed. G. Levine (New York, Oxford University Press, 1968), 230.

10. Charles Darwin, *Autobiography,* ed. Nora Barlow (London, Collins, 1958), 90. Cf. Donald Fleming, "Charles Darwin, the Anaesthetic Man," *VS,* 4 (1960-1961), 230f.

11. Ellegård, *Darwin,* 123f., 130f., 136., 139f.; GHL, "Mr. Darwin's Hypotheses," *FR,* n.s. 3:616 (June 1, 1868).

12. GHL, "Journal," Jan. 1, 1860 (*MS.* Beinecke Library).

13. *Animal Life,* 99, 110. Lewes did not use the term "hypostatisation," but he was acutely aware of the dangers of classifying and making distinctions, and then treating these classifications and distinctions as "real" (*Problems,* II, 434, 444).

14. "Spontaneous Generation." *Blackwood's,* 89:165f. (Feb. 1861); Ellegård, *Darwin,* 110.

15. *Animal Life,* 122; and cf. *ibid.,* 95.

16. H. Spencer, *An Autobiography* (2 vols., New York, D. Appleton and Company, 1904), I, 448; GHL's review of Adam Sedgwick's *Discourse on the Studies of the University of Cambridge,* in the *Leader,* 1:

566f. (Sept. 7, 1850), and of R. S. Wyld, *The Philosophy of the Senses,* in *ibid.,* 4:43 (Jan. 8, 1853).

17. J. A. Passmore, "Darwin and the Climate of Opinion," *Australian Journal of Science,* 22 (1959), 11; "Mr. Darwin's Hypotheses," *FR,* n.s. 3: 356, 612, and n.s. 4: 498; Ellegård, *Darwin,* 28f., 242f.

18. *Ibid.,* 185, 183. For a modern defense of the "hypothetico-deductive scientific method" as employed by Darwin, see M. Ghiselin, *The Triumph of the Darwinian Method* (Berkeley, University of California Press, 1969). S. J. Gould offers a fascinating description of an instance in which Darwin employed such a method and concludes that, in this case at least, "any pure empiricist would have surrendered to confusion long before 1859" ("Trigonia and the Origin of Species," *Journal of the History of Biology,* 1 [1968], 41-56).

19. Review of *Familiar Letters on Chemistry* in *Leader,* 2:682 (July 19, 1851); "Goethe," *WR,* 58:491 (Oct. 1852); *Sea-side Studies,* 206; *Problems,* I, 289.

20. "Mr. Darwin's Hypotheses," *FR,* n.s. 3:372-373.

21. *Ibid.,* n.s. 4:63-65. Lewes was commenting on Agassiz's 1859 *Essays on Classification;* of Claude Bernard, Lewes spoke in generally appreciative terms.

22. "Mr. Darwin's Hypotheses," *FR,* n.s. 4:493f., 501f.

23. Ellegård, *Darwin,* 294, 306, 311.

24. *Problems,* I, 152f., 156f. Lewes' summary in his "Diary" for 1871 (MS, Beinecke Library) noted "intense enjoyment" and "enlargement of insight" through his "first real study of mathematics"; cf. *Problems,* I, 124.

25. For a succinct discussion of Hutton's views, see A. W. Brown, *The Metaphysical Society: Victorian Minds in Crisis, 1869-1880* (New York, Columbia University Press, 1947), 44-46. For the Darwinian reply, see Ellegård, *Darwin,* 327.

26. *Problems,* IV, 41, 79, 165; I, 173. (See the Bibliographical Essay for an explanation of references to *Problems.*)

27. *Problems,* I, 158, 168, 239, 480f., 468.

28. *Ibid.,* V, 495.

29. *Ibid.,* V, vi, 108, 81.

30. *Ibid.,* III, 413, 409, and *passim.*

31. Owsei Temkin, "Materialism in French and German Physiology of the Early Nineteenth Century," *Bulletin of the History of Medicine,* 20 (1946), 322-324; GHL review of Beale, et al., *Physiological Anatomy,* in *FR,* 6:765 (Nov. 1, 1866). Cf. *Problems,* I, 110; III, 17, 22f.

32. *Problems,* IV, 74; I, 128.

33. "Spiritualism and Materialism," pt. 1, *FR,* n.s. 19:481f., 492f. (April 1876); pt. 2, *ibid.:* 717ff. (June 1876).

34. *Problems,* II, 3, 6; cf. *Sea-side Studies,* 53; R. H. Hutton, "Mr. Spencer on Moral Intuitions," *Contemporary Review,* 17 (1871), 464.

35. "On the Dread and Dislike of Science," *FR,* n.s. 23:812-815 (June 1878).

36. J. T. Merz, *A History of European Thought in the Nineteenth Century* (4 vols., New York, Dover Publications, 1965 reprint of a work originally published 1904-1912), III, 220; J. A. Passmore, *A Hundred Years of Philosophy* (2nd ed., London, Gerald Duckworth, 1966), 477.

37. GHL, *A Biographical History of Philosophy* (4 vols., London, 1845-1846), IV, 233.

38. Walter Houghton, *The Victorian Frame of Mind* (New Haven, Yale University Press, 1957), 14; GHL, review of Spencer's *Principles of Psychology,* in *SR,* 1:352f. (March 1, 1856). Cf. E. Cassirer, *The Problem of Knowledge: Philosophy, Science, and History since Hegel* (New Haven, Yale University Press, 1950), 15.

39. H. B. Acton, "Comte's Positivism and the Science of Society," *Philosophy,* 26 (1951), 294-296; L. Levy-Bruhl, *The Philosophy of Auguste Comte,* authorized translation with introduction by Frederic Harrison (New York, G. Putnam and Sons, 1903), 66.

40. *FR,* 3:128 (Nov. 15, 1865); 5:245 (June 1, 1866); *Problems,* I, i, 5f.

41. The only extended study of Lewes' philosophy to date is G. B. Grassi-Bertazzi, *Esame critico della filosofia di G. H. Lewes* (Messina, 1906), 23-26. Anthony Quinton ("Neglect of Victorian Philosophy," *VS,* 1 [1957-1958], 254) argues that "British idealism is especially interesting as a social phenomenon, as a conscience-stricken reaction against the heathen and vulgar complacency about material progress." Cf. Passmore, *Hundred Years,* ch. 3.

42. Jacques Loeb, *The Mechanistic Conception of Life,* ed. Donald Fleming (Cambridge, Mass., Harvard University Press, 1964), Introduction, viii, ix.

43. *Biographical History,* III, 147; and see above, ch. 1 and n. 26.

44. "Spinoza," *FR,* 4:399 (April 1, 1866).

45. *Biographical History,* III, 148-150, 156-158.

46. *Ibid.,* IV, 97; "Thoughts for the Thoughtful," *Monthly Repository,* 1:57 (Jan. 1, 1838); *Biographical History,* III, 4.

47. *Leader,* 4:111 (Jan. 29, 1853); *Biographical History,* III, 4, 6f.

48. *Ibid.,* 72, 75.

49. *Ibid.,* 196, 212f.

50. *Problems,* I, 3-6. Cf. Lewes' critical review of Harriet Martineau and H. G. Atkinson, *Letters on Man's Nature and Development,* in *Leader,* 49:201-203 (March 1, 1851).

51. *BFR,* 15 (1843), 353-406.

52. Noel Annan, "The Curious Strength of Positivism in English

Political Thought," in *Hobhouse Memorial Lectures 1951-1960* (London, Athlone Press, 1962). See also Leszek Kolakowski, *The Alienation of Reason* (New York, Doubleday, 1968) for a succinct and authoritative account of positivist thought; Passmore, *Hundred Years,* 13; Cassirer, *Problem of Knowledge,* 7; F. A. Hayek, "Comte and Hegel," *Measure,* 2 (1951), 330.

53. J. Kaines, *Seven Lectures on the Doctrine of Positivism* (London, 1880), 5f.

54. Comte to GHL, Jan. 28, 1847 (MS, Archives Positivistes, Paris). Cf. E. M. Everett, *The Party of Humanity: The Fortnightly Review and Its Contributors, 1865-1874* (Chapel Hill, University of North Carolina Press, 1939), 86.

55. M. M. Bevington, *The Saturday Review, 1855-1868: Representative Educated Opinion in Victorian England* (New York, Columbia University Press, 1941), 254, 258; W. M. Simon, "Auguste Comte's English Disciples," *VS,* 8 (1964-1965), 172; F. S. Marvin, "Frederic Harrison," *Isis,* 6 (1924), 387-390.

56. *Problems,* I, 62, 65, 67f., 84f.

57. *Ibid.,* 29-33, 35f., 47.

58. J. H. Muirhead, "How Hegel Came to England," *Mind,* 36 (1927), 435; O. Chadwick, *The Victorian Church,* vol. I (London, A. and C. Black, 1966), 567f.

59. *Problems,* I, 18, 249-251; II, 442.

60. *Ibid.,* I, 357; II, 361, 376, 392.

61. "Niebuhr and the Classical Museum," *WR,* 41 (1844), 179; "Reign of Law," *FR,* n.s. 2 (1867), 109.

62. *Problems,* II, 229, 310.

63. *Ibid.,* I, 89, 94, 106, 193; II, 88. On Uniformitarianism, see Gillispie, *Genesis and Geology,* 131, and Ellegård, *Darwin,* 289; and cf. *ibid.,* 118; on the "universality of natural causation": J. W. Burrow, *Evolution and Society* (Cambridge University Press, 1966), 107-109.

64. A. Bain, "The Uniformity of Nature," *Mind,* 1 (1876), 146; Lewes' reply: *ibid.,* 282; cf. *Problems,* I, 397f., 408; S. J. Gould, "Is Uniformitarianism Necessary?" *American Journal of Science,* 263 (1965), 223-228.

65. *Problems,* II, 200, 212-214.

66. Alexandre Koyre, *From the Closed World to the Infinite Universe* (Baltimore, Johns Hopkins University Press, 1957); Acton, "Comte's Positivism," 300.

67. *Problems,* I, 82, 348; II, 437; "Goethe as a Man of Science," *WR,* 58:484 (Oct. 1852); "Life and Doctrine of Geoffroy-St. Hilaire," *ibid.,* 61: 171, 177 (Jan. 1854). Lewes became more sympathetic to Kant and Hegel in the seventies, especially in *Problems.*

68. *Problems,* I, 241, 416f.; II, 11, 15; *Animal Life,* 61.

69. *Problems,* I, 185, 209, 224-228, 368, 376, 385.

70. *Ibid.,* I, 292, 168. The example of the tides had previously been used by Mill in his *System of Logic* (1843).

71. *Problems,* I, 304f., 456f.

72. *Ibid.,* 103; II, 61.

73. *Ibid.,* I, 49, 170ff.

74. *Ibid.,* 341, 315.

75. *Ibid.,* II, 30; I, 22.

76. *Ibid.,* I, 182f., 201; II, 441.

77. *Ibid.,* II, 426, 493.

78. See *ibid.,* I, 73, where Lewes discusses Hegel's objective logic.

79. Bertrand Russell, *A History of Western Philosophy* (New York, Simon and Schuster, 1945), 591.

80. F. Harrison, "The Positivist Problem," *FR,* n.s. 6:471, 472 (Nov. 1, 1869); GHL, "Comte and Mill," *FR,* 6 (1866), 387f.; *Problems,* I, 21.

Epilogue

1. R. L. Brett, "George Henry Lewes, Dramatist, Novelist and Critic," in *Essays and Studies,* 11 (1958), 101-120.

2. George Eliot, *Middlemarch,* chs. 3 and 22; John Gross, *The Rise and Fall of the Man of Letters* (London, Weidenfeld and Nicolson, 1969), 74f.

3. H. Spencer, *Autobiography* (2 vols., New York, D. Appleton and Company, 1904), I, 437; E. L. Linton, *My Literary Life* (London, 1899), 26.

Index

169

HARVARD HISTORICAL MONOGRAPHS

41. The Urban Frontier: The Rise of Western Cities, 1790-1830. By Richard C. Wade. 1959.

42. New Zealand, 1769-1840: Early Years of Western Contact. By Harrison M. Wright. 1959.

44. Foch versus Clemenceau: France and German Dismemberment, 1918-1919. By Jere Clemens King. 1960.

46. Carroll Wright and Labor Reform: The Origin of Labor Statistics. By James Leiby. 1960.

47. Chōshū in the Meiji Restoration. By Albert M. Craig. 1961.

48. John Fiske: The Evolution of a Popularizer. By Milton Berman. 1961.

49. John Jewel and the Problem of Doctrinal Authority. By W. M. Southgate. 1962.

50. Germany and the Diplomacy of the Financial Crisis, 1931. By Edward W. Bennett. 1962.

51. Public Opinion, Propaganda, and Politics in Eighteenth-Century England: A Study of the Jew Bill of 1753. By Thomas W. Perry. 1962.

52. Soldier and Civilian in the Later Roman Empire. By Ramsay MacMullen. 1963.

53. Copyhold, Equity, and the Common Law. By Charles Montgomery Gray. 1963.

54. The Association: British Extraparliamentary Political Association, 1769-1793. By Eugene Charlton Black. 1963.

55. Tocqueville and England. By Seymour Drescher. 1964.

56. Germany and the Emigration, 1816-1885. By Mack Walker. 1964.

57. Ivan Aksakov (1823-1886): A Study in Russian Thought and Politics. By Stephen Lukashevich. 1965.

58. The Fall of Stein. By R. C. Raack. 1965.

59. The French Apanages and the Capetian Monarchy, 1224-1328. By Charles T. Wood. 1966.

60. Congressional Insurgents and the Party System, 1909-1916. By James Holt. 1967.

61. The Rumanian National Movement in Transylvania, 1780-1849. By Keith Hitchins. 1969.

62. Sisters of Liberty: Marseille, Lyon, Paris and the Reaction to a Centralized State, 1868-1871. By Louis M. Greenberg. 1971.